Ruth Wilkerson Harris

# The Wilkerson Legacy

The Compelling Story of the Courageous Family that
Birthed Teen Challenge

by

Ruth Wilkerson Harris

Unless otherwise stated all scriptures are taken from the King
James Version (KJV) Some scripture quotations were taken
from the Amplified® Bible, Copyright © 1954, 1958, 1962,
1964, 1965, 1987 by The Lockman Foundation.
Used by permission."

Published by
VMI Publishers
Sisters, Oregon
www.vmipublishers.com

ISBN 0-9747190-5-6
Library of Congress Control Number:  2005926290

To Contact Author, email:
RUTHWHARRIS@aol.com

# CONTENTS

# ACKNOWLEDGEMENTS

The Wilkerson Legacy could not be told without stories given to me in writing from Maxine Wilkerson, Gillam Lyon, and Aunt Gertha Dengler; or without input from Aunt Elaine Eslinger and Hilda Leach, Gertha's only daughter. And, of course, I gained a wealth of knowledge from my family, visits with Fay Mianulli, and by observing, listening, and recording. I thank my brother, Don, who gave me encouragement to write our story, telling me: "It's your story of our family— write how you see it."

The story would never be in print without VMI publisher, Bill Carmichael, who believed The Wilkerson Legacy was an important one to pass on. Lacey Hanes-Ogle, who insisted that "this story must be told," gave me valuable suggestions, and Barbara Haas patiently corrected punctuation and spelling to make this the best manuscript possible.

Without the encouragement of my children and my husband, I might have given up when voices of discouragement sounded in my ear.

Yes, I am telling it as I know it, but it is, after all, a family history. For this reason, I am donating all the proceeds of the book to Global Teen Challenge and The Helper Ministry.

# PROLOGUE

I am not a historian, but I have personally collected the stories of four generations of the Wilkerson family that will be shared in this book. As a member of the family, I have been profoundly affected by the lives and beliefs of those around me and those who have gone before me. I want to tell the story of our family because of the strong spiritual legacy they have given us, and also because I believe that every generation needs to hear the stories of families who have gone before them; they need to know the people who trusted God and were trusted by God to build His Kingdom on earth.

We are an ordinary family tree made up of farmers, miners, trolley operators, and on every family branch you will find preachers.

There is a common experience shared by all of us: the sense of being a "called" people. Some family members have been more aware than others of this common thread weaving its way through all the generations, but when it is heard and answered, we have each set out to answer the calling with a strong determination to fulfill our mission.

Whether the call was to America to settle in the Cumberland Mountains of Tennessee, or to defend our nation, or to preach from pulpits in tents, in sanctuaries, and on the streets—or to live righteously in our homes and in a worldly society, we are sure when God calls, we are to follow.

## Chapter 1

# THE PIONEERS

I would like to brag that our adventurous forefather arrived on the Mayflower, but alas, I must confess, I was unable to trace the date, or ship or port of arrival. I do know that our English ancestors heard the call from the pulpits and the printed page in their homeland to pioneer farms in a southern state of a young nation. Who could resist a promise land advertised to have lofty mountains with crystal clear rivers and streams that carry fertile soil into the valleys, land well adapted for pasturage and the production of an abundance of food, and friendly neighbors who had come to America with the same hopes and dreams?

My ancestors had heard of another group of people who long ago were called to a land flowing with milk and honey and they too decided to follow God's call even though they knew there would be trials to endure. With God's help, they knew they would prosper. And so it happened on the Wilkerson portion of American land located near Maynardville, Tennessee, that the foundation of a farm began to take shape in the 1800s. The log cabin began as a wood-framed house of several rooms and later progressed to a two-story farmhouse.

At the crossroads of the community stood a small church, the gathering place for worship and all their social activities. Religious freedom, with a Baptist influence, abounded in the seclusion of the Cumberland Mountains. The Wilkersons were happy to be American settlers who could live and worship without being mocked for their beliefs.

A son was born in 1844 and christened Jackson, a patriotic choice to honor Andrew Jackson. From an early age, it was evident he had inherited the same adventurous spirit as his father and his namesake.

When the Civil War broke out between the North and South in 1861, the Wilkersons found themselves at odds with some of their neighbors. It was their belief that God had placed His blessing upon the young nation. Jackson's family believed that God expected them to remain loyal to the country. The seventeen-year-old agreed with his family that Tennessee should not secede from the Union. Without the blessings of his parents, he decided to do his part to keep the nation united. He left home to find the nearest Union recruitment center in the county. No questions were asked about his age—both men and boys were being recruited to defend the nation.

Jackson joined the Union Volunteer Army and was assigned to Company A, 2nd Tennessee Infantry. Only a few months later, he was taken prisoner by the southern Confederate army. The divided loyalties within his home state had pitted neighbor against neighbor. The life of adventure young Jackson had dreamed of had turned into a horrible experience, one that would leave physical scars and eventually cause an early death at the age of forty-one.

The Civil War ended in April of 1865. For Jackson, freedom came a few weeks after the truce when news of the truce reached the camp. The very next month, Jackson and his childhood sweetheart, Sarah Jane Lynch Selvidge, were united in marriage. Together they set about doing their part to plant and replenish the war-torn state. Sarah worked side-by-side with her husband, mending fences and barns until things were back in order on the Wilkerson homestead. And they did their part to enlarge the population of Union County.

Into their brood of eight children, a handsome baby boy was born on May 22, 1883. His parents proudly named him James Arthur Garfield after President Garfield and his running mate, Chester Arthur. My grandfather captured the spotlight from the moment he was born and never stepped out of it. The only tragedy that marred his entrance into the world was his father's choice of his patriotic name. Unfortunately, having the name of a Yankee-born president in the South had a catastrophic influence on his youngest son, as it brought him nothing but ridicule throughout his youth. At a young age, James Arthur insisted on the nickname "J.A." and never again acknowledged the name Garfield.

His older brothers, long since over the sting of being called Yankee-lovers, laughed at their younger brother getting worked up over insults hollered back and forth by the young Confederate crowd. It didn't take J.A. long to come to his own defense without the help of unreliable reinforcements.

"Hey, Garfoot," the sons of neighboring farmers would call. "What's the son of a Yankee-lover doing livin' down in Rebel country?"

"You call me that name again and I'll punch your nose flatter than a buttermilk biscuit." J.A. wished he'd hurry up and be "grow'd up" so he would be able to carry out his threat.

That day quickly came. Soon there was hardly a boy in the county who hadn't felt the affects of his threats. He listened to enough teasing about his name and flattened more than a few noses. With a quick fist and a sure-fired barrage of fighting words, he settled the war with neighboring kids.

Throughout Granddad's life, he kept on the winning team thanks to the women in his life—especially his mother. Sarah knew how to keep young J.A. walking the straight and narrow path as long as he lived at home.

After his father died in 1885, J.A. soon learned that he had to accept responsibility, even at his young age, if the Wilkerson family intended to stay together. Sarah wasn't about to give up just because her husband died leaving her with young children. Much too proud to beg or borrow, she rallied her assets around her and put a plan into effect. She enforced a work schedule, defying anyone of her brood to disobey her orders, and that included the youngest.

With Spartan tactics she maneuvered her small company into accomplishing feats that most Southern women left to hired hands. From morning to night she issued orders and like a good General, she led her troops through each accomplishment. There were no slackers on the Wilkerson farm and no one dared to go AWOL.

Because J.A. was only two when his father died, he wasn't able to attend school for long. He was needed on the farm after his older brothers married and left to build their own homes. J.A. left school with no intention of taking instructions from a schoolmarm again.

Being a dropout at an early age never seriously affected him. His motto, "Experience is the best teacher," served him well in decision making throughout his life. He wasn't averse to book learning, but it would be many years after the day he had closed the door of the little one-room schoolhouse in the Tennessee mountains before he would admit that he needed more schooling. One thing was certain—he never had trouble matching wits with anyone he met, either in business or in the ministry.

Sarah and her little army became quite successful as farmers. Her early morning drills with instructions for precision planting and a constant watch over the fields yielded abundant harvests. J.A. bragged all his life about the hundreds of bushels he filled with green beans. Every week during the summer months, J.A. would accompany his older brothers to the Knoxville Market Square where the green beans he had picked sold for the great sum of twenty-five cents a bushel.

When her children reached the age where she could no longer use the rod, Sarah applied her own homespun philosophy. J.A. told a story, with noticeable satisfaction, about the time his older brother, Will, learned a lesson through one of his mother's home remedies.

According to J.A., Will was the sneaky one of the bunch. He had a girl who lived several farms away and every Friday night he would get slicked up for his date. No one could vouch for the time of Will's return, but J.A. was positive it wasn't on the same day he had headed off down the road.

Since Will couldn't do without his sleep, he was forced to sneak a few winks between plowing fields. His catnaps often lasted through the morning and Sarah began to notice the fields weren't up to par.

"Now what do you suppose a General like my mother could do with a great big fellow like my brother Will?" J.A. would ask his audience, his eyes sparkling with mischievous glee, as if he was seeing it happen all over again.

Sarah knew better than to lecture, and she certainly couldn't court-martial Will. She pondered the situation for a while, keeping the others in suspense about how she would punish their big brother. Sarah said not a word. That evening while the children slept, Sarah got out a clean pair of underwear for Will and neatly laid it out where he would easily find it and be sure to put it on—but not before she rubbed the inside with a hot pepper fresh from the garden.

In the morning when the younger children left for the fields, Will, wearing his clean underwear, sleepily followed them out. About high noon, Sarah left the house for an inspection tour. She headed right for Will's territory. Just as she suspected, Will had found a comfortable spot to sleep.

"Only he wasn't exactly napping," J.A. would say with a roar of laughter. "There he was, the hot sun burning him up, but not as much as that hot pepper! He squirmed, he scratched, he rubbed and he swore, but nothing stopped Mother's home remedy from doing its job."

Sarah surprised Will with a thrash of her walking stick and gave him a scolding like he had never heard before and hoped never to hear again. As J.A. put it, "Will was 'itching' to get away from Ma, but he was in no position to get out of Ma's tirade until she had exhausted her anger."

Unlike Will, J.A. was too busy living to sleep his life away. Occasionally, he took time off from farming to see the world around him. On one of his trips, he discovered the square dance and the fiddle players. "I took a hankering to music, bought myself a banjo, sat on Ma's front porch and learned to play." It was as simple as that with J.A. —when he wanted to do something, he did it. Before long, you could find him most Saturday nights playing his banjo at the local square dances.

On one occasion, J.A. dressed for the occasion as usual with his only Sunday trousers pressed to perfection, his one white shirt starched so stiff it could stand alone, his black wavy hair slicked back with the latest brand of hair oil, and took off down the road with his banjo under his arm, whistling the latest dance tunes.

"James Arthur Garfield." J.A. stopped suddenly in his tracks; he was sure he heard someone call him by "that" name. "Who'd dare?" he wondered. He looked around, trying to pierce the darkness—not a soul was in sight. Thinking he had only imagined the voice, J.A. started off again, only this time a little more cautiously. "James Arthur Garfield," the voice said distinctly. J.A. stopped with a jolt, his hair standing on end; dropping his banjo he swung his body around with fists ready to strike, but no one stood ready to charge. Through the eerie quietness came the voice: "I want you to preach the Gospel." The voice seemed to come from above.

Calmly he pushed his hair back into place, picked up his instrument from the road, stood his full six-foot-two inches, looked up toward the star-filled sky and in firm tones said: "God,

I'd rather die first than preach the Gospel." Hoping this was his final contact with God about such nonsense, J.A. stalked off, still whistling, anticipating a great deal more excitement.

Now J.A. didn't doubt for a minute that the voice had been God's. His mother had brought up each one of her children in the knowledge of the Scriptures. If God had talked to the people in Bible times, he expected God could call His name if He wanted to, he just couldn't understand why God would call him to be a preacher.

J.A. readily acknowledged that he'd received a call, but the idea of exchanging his fun-loving way of life for a pious life that seemed to be a trademark for all the parsons he'd ever met was unbearable. After J.A. told God where he stood on the matter, he simply forgot about God's proposition and went on with his life. It would be some time before he would remember the words he had heard on the road that night.

The more important voice in J.A.'s life was that of a petite Southern belle he had met at a square dance. Della Kitts, just sixteen, attended the dances to meet friends. She had been orphaned at a young age and raised by her grandfather. She dreamed of the kind of man she hoped to marry, and determined he had to be a Christian. When she met J.A., she knew she had fallen in love. J.A. looked into her dark brown eyes and right on the spot he boldly informed Della, "We're going to get married."

J.A. had been thinking for some time about marriage. At seventeen he knew neither the farm nor his mother could support his worldly ambitions. Thoughts of going off alone didn't appeal to him at all. He liked a woman's touch in his life, especially since he preferred to remain ignorant about such things as taking care of his clothes, cooking a meal or cleaning a room. J.A. did well socially, crowds were his delight and he liked being in the middle, dominating the conversation. But he knew he could not function without a woman's help.

J.A. proposed and marriage vows were exchanged on August

23, 1901, before the Baptist minister at the Wilkerson homestead in Union County.

Not for a minute did J.A. worry about the responsibility he ardently embraced as husband at a young age. No challenge bothered him at that moment of his life. For that matter, no challenge ever seemed too great for him to accept. J.A. had an indomitable will to take action even if his ideas didn't please anyone. As long as he thought his decisions seemed a good idea, he plunged ahead with not much thought about the outcome. Somehow his plans turned out for good—but not always.

Sarah had wondered if getting married was the right thing for her youngest son to do. She couldn't imagine her mischievous son settling down to become a husband and father, but she had underestimated the five-foot-three, fiery-eyed Della. She promptly took over where Sarah left off.

J.A. quickly assumed responsibility for his bride by taking a job in a local icehouse, but the salary did not meet their needs. Against Della's protests, he took a job in the Fraterville coalmines in an adjoining county. He hated and feared the dangerous work of digging coal in underground tunnels that the miners knew were unsafe. Yet it provided money for a small rental house and food for the table.

On the morning of May 19, 1902, Della and J.A. woke to the loud ringing of the alarm clock. The clock stopped abruptly. It seemed to dance right off the dresser, smashing into a dozen pieces as it hit the floor. Della took this as a bad omen and begged J.A. not to go to the mines. He listened to his wife's warning. Early that afternoon an explosion ripped through the mine, killing 239 men. It is said to have been the worst southern mine disaster in the history of America.

J.A. did go to the mines that day to help in the rescue of trapped men and console families—many women lost their husbands and their sons in the explosion. He determined never to go back into the work of mining and made the decision to seek employment in Knoxville.

Living in a population of 25,000 people and the largest city in eastern Tennessee, J.A. was confident he would find a new career. J.A. and Della were extremely pleased with J.A.'s new job as a conductor on the City Traction Trolley Company. Della was certain that God had guided them to live in the city and had provided a good career for J.A. She looked forward to new experiences and new blessings.

The greatest surprise for his mother was the news that J.A. was attending church with Della. Sarah felt reassured. She knew her youngest would turn out all right. For all she knew Della might even persuade J.A. to answer the call.

## CHAPTER 2

# OPERATION J.A.

Della said she married J.A. for two reasons: first, because he was a Baptist, and second, because he was tall and handsome. She was not ashamed to admit she had lost her heart, but she wanted to make it clear to her debonair husband that she had not lost her religion.

"This is the way it is, Dear—God first and you second," Della announced to J.A. She assumed every religious couple lived the way she had been taught; of course, she expected her husband to readily agree with her Christian ideals of marriage.

J.A. easily followed in the religious path of his wife. He regularly attended church on Sunday, and he especially enjoyed the church dinners. After eating good food, he delighted in gathering a crowd around him to tell his experiences—which were often embellished to give his audiences a dramatic version of the stories.

On September 23, 1904, a daughter was born. Both parents were delighted. Della had lost her first child at birth, so baby Gertha was a special gift from God. J.A. hoped for a son to complete the family. When Kenneth, the image of his father, was born on April 6, 1906, they were ecstatic. Yes, Della could say that God had abundantly blessed her marriage.

All was not well, however. After a year of city living, Della noticed a reversal in J.A.'s priorities. He began spending more time with his friends at the trolley barn, and soon a disturbing change in her husband's behavior became too obvious to ignore. She was sure J.A. had been snared into the sins of drinking and gambling with his buddies. With J.A. it was self first, family second, and somewhere down the line God could find his place. As you can imagine, this did not set well with Della! She had to do something to show her husband the error of his ways. Della quickly approached God with a plan to snare the soul of J.A. from the tempter. It took a bit of work, but the end result was the triumph of one woman's faith and persistence in prayer.

"Operation J.A." began on a warm night. Della talked J.A. into taking a walk around the city square. In the center of the town they came upon a group of men and women holding some sort of street meeting. J.A. had a nose for anything religious; he could detect a church meeting a mile away. He jerked his wife's arm to steer her in the opposite direction, but already her ears had perked up at the sound of voices singing hymns.

Excitedly, she tugged on her husband's coat sleeve, pulling him through the crowd right to a prime spot in the front row. She seemed oblivious to J.A.'s aggravation. Completely enthralled by the enthusiastic singing and testimonies of salvation and healing, Della stood watching, fascinated with the street meeting. Her husband's mounting agitation went unnoticed. Shifting from one foot to another, J.A. frantically looked for a way to escape.

Just then the Main Street trolley came clanging down the tracks. J.A. momentarily had thoughts of taking a freedom ride.

"Hey, Wilkerson," the motorman shouted above the singing. "What are you doing with that bunch?" And he let out a loud guffaw pointing his finger at the gathering. Being forced by his wife to be a reluctant bystander was mortifying enough, but the humiliation of being associated with a religious street meeting was too much for J.A.

"My God, Della. Let's get out of here," he whispered. He

got a firm grip on his wife's arm and pulled her away from the gathering, forcing her to keep up with his long strides until he had assumed a safe distance. Sweat poured down his forehead. Loosening the stiff collar around his neck, J.A. heaved a loud sigh of relief. "Now that's all I'll hear down at the trolley barn in the morning!"

"James Arthur! What do you mean by pulling me away when I wanted to listen? There's nothing wrong with those people. They were only trying to tell about the wonderful miracles God has done for them. I think their testimonies were marvelous. Oh, how I'd like to testify like they did! We never hear anything like that in our church."

"Thank God for small favors," J.A. mumbled in a selfish prayer. He felt his wife's fervent religion was sufficient for them both. He reckoned she had enough faith to get them through heaven's pearly gates and made a mental note not to take a stroll on Saturday evenings.

The next day Della inquired about the folks conducting the street services and learned that they were meeting in neighborhood prayer meetings to pray for revival and for sinners. She knocked on doors on her own street and soon found what she was seeking. The women welcomed Della to their prayer group. She accepted the invitation without hesitation. Already in her heart, she anticipated new blessings from God and angels rejoicing over a certain sinner repenting of his sins.

She returned from her first prayer meeting overflowing with joy. She was in awe of women who could pray the "prayer of faith" with a fervency she had never experienced. She was anxious to share the news with her church friends. She told them: "I believed the preachers who said the miraculous events of the early Church were not meant for this generation. I have now witnessed with my own eyes that this is not true."

Della was astounded to learn that revivals had been spreading throughout the United States. Many churches were being affected, but denominations as a whole went on record as stating that it was only an emotional demonstration put on by the uneducated. Glibly, they backed their derogatory statements by declaring that the miraculous acts of the Apostles and the gifts of the Holy Spirit pertained only to the first Church. From behind the pulpits, clergymen scoffed at the idea of modern miracles and the majority of congregations believed them.

The dispersions of some did not stop people from leaving their historical churches and joining thousands seeking a deeper spiritual experience rooted in and encouraged by the teachings of Jesus and the Apostles. The very idea that God would pour out His Spirit again was based on the Scriptures. If God is the same yesterday, today and forever, they reasoned, then why wouldn't He continue to empower the Church as He did in the days of the Apostles?

These earnest seekers met together in homes and rented buildings praying for a revival in their churches, unaware they were laying the foundation for a body of believers who would eventually spark a century-long revival in the very denominations that did not recognize a genuine work of the Holy Spirit.

Della's powerful Gospel was not forthcoming from the Pentecostals, but from a group seeking holiness. Their adherence to a strict code of ethics, morals and rules regarding outward appearance made them an oddity even in that day. In spite of their idiosyncrasies, they stood out as shining moral lights in a world filled with atheistic beliefs, and a society turning its back on godliness. The skeptical onlookers had to marvel at the simplicity of a faith that produced amazing results: town drunkards were delivered from addiction to alcohol, people were healed of diseases, and wayward sinners cried tears of repentance and became model citizens and caring family members.

Except one wayward sinner who saw no reason to repent!

When Della came home from these prayer meetings bursting with the zeal of the Lord, her husband pursed his lips as if in deep thought, shook his head in disbelief, and then shrugged his shoulders and dismissed his wife's religious fervor from his mind. But not for long! Her friends were right. Della had been fired up with an added dose of religion, and she expected her husband to accept the "full Gospel" that had become so clear to her.

J.A. had inherited a religion from his parents as they had from their parents. "If it was good enough for my parents, it's good enough for me," he boasted to Della. He wanted her to understand that his brand of religion, which didn't require too much change and did not expect miracles, perfectly suited him. He decided that ignoring his wife's latest religious fad would dampen her enthusiasm for an evangelistic campaign to change him.

He was wrong. Della talked incessantly about her new faith.

J.A. decided to try his powers of reasoning. J.A. was known for his own brand of highly successful psychology. He was a man of rare qualities, capable of a blunt diplomacy but void of real tact. He approached his wife with his gentlest tone, "Della, we aren't bad people. We go to church every Sunday. If it's prayer meetings you want, why can't you pray with the folks of our church? We can always use a bit of prayer."

Della had deliberately set out to break her proud, stubborn, and arrogant husband, and she didn't plan to do it diplomatically. She was not fooled for one minute by her husband's smooth approach. She was sharp enough to know that when J.A. said "we," he really meant "you."

With a rare show of ferocity, she attacked his false piety. "Goodness won't get you into heaven; and if anyone could use a bit of prayer, it's you, James Arthur Garfield." That double insult (Della only called him by his full name when she was angry) signaled a break off of diplomatic relations as far as J.A. was concerned. Now he would face her with the truth!

"Half the town thinks you've gone crazy, Della." He wanted to add his own feelings about his wife's present sanity, but from experience he knew better than to incur her wrath. "For the likes of me, I don't see why we have to change. If you want people to think you've gone batty, don't get me mixed up with such hogwash. I'll be damned if I ever join a bunch of idiots!"

If rewards were given out for stubbornness, my grandparents would have tied each other for first place. J.A. meant what he said that morning just as much as Della did. The battle charge had been called, the two sides had taken their positions and only surrender on the part of one of the sides could end the war. Della had no thought of weakening. She was on God's side!

Up to the day Della got involved with the "fanatics," J.A. had been content with his life. He loved his family; he even found comfort in church. On his job, however, fear had become an every day torment. The pain and stiffness in his legs from standing for hours at the helm of the trolley was not getting better. His buddies at the barn offered him alcohol as a solution for the pain. It seemed to work, but it also brought feelings of guilt. Della's religion took the blame for the drinking and the guilt.

Before long, J.A. preferred being with his drinking buddies more than with his wife and children. To add to his self-elevation, he had found favor with his boss and had earned a promotion. It seems he had formulated his own plan for exacting fares from people who thought the city should provide free transportation. The open-sided trolleys gave riders a good opportunity to slip out without paying. J.A. decided to carry a small black, pearl-handled pistol in full view of his passengers. It never failed to bring results. As a reward for his "bravery" the company promoted him to motorman.

The most popular trolley in town happened to be J.A.'s. He welcomed his passengers aboard, especially the ladies, as if they were boarding the Presidential Car. He kept their minds off the jolts and bounces with highly fictitious stories of his youthful escapades. J.A. became a hero to the children while the adults sat back listening with amusement to his endless stories of pranks and heroism.

His charismatic personality wasn't getting him anywhere with his wife, though, and neither was his fussing and fuming about her religion. His only relief from her persistence was staying away from home as much as possible. The trolley barn, a popular gambling house, became J.A.'s hangout. His newfound friends soon convinced him he needed their fellowship, so he joined the Odd Fellows. But his deeds brought much sorrow to Della; still, she trusted God, praying: "Lord, bring my husband to you at any cost."

To worsen matters, J.A.'s conscience troubled him. His wife's prayers brought back memories of her warnings not to go to work in the mine the day of the terrible explosion. His conscience had pricked him that day; he wondered why God had spared his life. His thoughts were also troubled with the memory of that night when he had dared to say: "God, I'd rather die than preach the Gospel."

Brushes with death seemed to be God's opportune time to remind J.A. of his call to work for the Kingdom of God, but J.A. kept responding with a resounding "no." He had left the mines with a hacking cough that reached the critical stage of pneumonia. The doctor gave no hope for his recovery. Only the prayers of his wife saved him, and he knew it, though wouldn't admit to it. Now, constantly standing while operating the trolley, he developed enlarged veins in his legs and not even the rubber stockings that he faithfully wore could relieve the aching.

Not long after Della prayed for his salvation "at any cost," J.A. had his third bout with death. Even Della became alarmed. "Lord, this isn't what I meant." But God knew the way to J.A.'s heart.

This time it was news that came from Dr. West, the family physician, and it wasn't good. "J.A., you've got galloping consumption and there's not much I can do for you. Your only hope is to move to a drier climate." J.A. just couldn't bring himself to believe the doctor. "It will wear off. I'm strong. I'll outlive you, Doc."

He secretly wished for a small portion of his wife's faith, but he was too proud to admit he needed God and too proud to identify himself as a sinner. His stubbornness had a price tag. His left leg had become so stiff he could barely walk, his stomach so full of ulcers he could not eat a full meal, and his constant cough left him in a weakened condition; yet he rejected the prayers of his wife to settle his account with God, still searching for another remedy.

On the advice of a friend, J.A. began to use a remedy of corn whiskey and rock candy. At first it took just a little to boost his strength, but soon he found he needed more to satisfy the desire for liquor he had acquired. This new remedy showed no signs of improving his health or his disposition, and it only worsened his faltering spiritual condition.

It took the grace of God for Della to live with him, yet her faith stood firm. She had prayed the prayer of relinquishment and meant it—there would be no more lectures. She only wished the cost had not brought her husband to his present pitiful state. She never knew in what condition he would come home. Often it was in a drunken stupor, causing the devil in him to lash out at his wife and her religion.

He relented of his evil deeds almost as soon as he committed them and tried to make amends with peace offerings, the last of which was a beautiful sixteen-ribbed umbrella. Della had no intentions of accepting peace offerings in place of repentance. She swept the umbrella out of her husband's hands, shouting, "James Arthur Garfield, the Bible declares it is better to obey than to sacrifice" and proceeded to break the gift over his head. Never again did J.A. bring home a peace offering!

Della believed a price must be paid for everything in life—the greater the value, the greater the cost. Yet, she was unprepared for her husband's decision to move to a northern state. His excuse was to work in a better climate, but his real desire was to go on ahead of Della and the children to temporarily escape the prayers of his wife and her fanatical friends.

Little did he realize those very prayers would follow him every mile he journeyed to Danville, Illinois. All the devils in hell couldn't stop Della's prayers from reaching their destination. It took only three weeks for God to bring about His next confrontation with James Arthur Wilkerson. That's how long it took J.A. to make the decision to attend his first holiness revival.

## CHAPTER 3

# HOUNDED BY HEAVEN

After settling into a boarding house in Danville, J.A. applied for a job with the trolley company that had been recommended to him by his boss in Knoxville. Then he looked for a saloon to quench his thirst for alcohol. Surprisingly, it was while sitting in the saloon he heard gossip about an unusual tent revival.

The tent meeting in the nearby community of Georgetown was the current attraction in Danville. J.A. had no intentions of putting himself at risk with a holiness crowd, but it seemed the entire population attended for one reason or another. Curious by nature and having nothing better to do, J.A. made his way to the Nazarene tent revival one night.

He entered the tent cautiously, fully intending to play the role of critic. He quickly scanned the tent for a back seat from which to view the "show." Hands seemed to rush out to give him a hearty welcome. J.A. thought his arm would shake off. "Here, brother. Let me find you a good seat."

He tried to inform the kind man that he wasn't his brother, but the firm hand on his back pushed him down the aisle to a front bench. As soon as he slumped into the seat another "brother" approached from the front and thrust a paperback songbook into his hands.

Then a voice boomed through the tent: "Everybody raise your voice to God and SING." And did they sing! J.A., unprepared for such exuberance in a religious service, quickly got caught up in the lively music. He wished he had brought his banjo.

Forgetting his role of critic, he listened in spite of his arrogant intentions. Granddad talked about the first holiness revival he attended for many years afterward.

The evangelist read the text taken from Matthew 5:29-30. J.A. thought that the sermon about plucking an eye out and cutting off an arm seemed terribly harsh. Then with great fervency, the preacher thundered out a list of sins needing to be "plucked out and cut off," until the audience shuddered in their seats at the awfulness of their thoughts and deeds. J.A. cringed down in his seat. The preacher stormed out the words of Christ: "Pluck it out, cut it off!" Dramatically, he thrust his hand to his eye as if to pluck his own out and J.A. thought for sure he heard the preacher's eyeball hit the floor. He caught his feet up for fear it might roll and stop right at his seat. Never had the Scriptures been made so powerful.

J.A. made a quick escape out of the side of the tent with a sigh of relief. The reality of the message haunted him long after his escape, but something compelled him to return for more attacks on his self-righteous Christianity.

Again J.A. sat trembling in his seat as the words of the evangelist uncovered his innermost thoughts and deeds. Again he hastily made his escape from the watchful eyes of the "brothers" who urged sinners to the mourner's bench.

J.A. was back for the third night. This time, he waited outside for a group of folks with whom he could slip into the tent to avoid the handshakes. He was sure they could see conviction written all over his face. His heart pounded so loudly it frightened him. He, J.A. Wilkerson, fearless of any man, was being shaken by the words of a holiness evangelist.

The night's message on the return of Christ for His Church alarmed J.A. who had never thought of Christ returning to earth.

In sonorous tones, the evangelist rolled out warnings of hell, fire and brimstone. He took his audience to hell, back to earth, and then on through the gates of Heaven.

J.A. got as far as hell. He thought he felt the fires of hell licking about his feet. Soon it felt like his trousers had caught fire! The voice made a pleading call for sinners to come forward. He half stood, gasping for air. "God, I'm one of those sinners," he cried out in anguish as he stumbled to the altar. In that instance, all J.A.'s pride, his stubbornness, and arrogance melted under the scrutinizing eye of the Holy Spirit. In that instant, the angels rejoiced, for a sinner had come home!

J.A. got up from that mourner's bench a new person. He felt liberated, as if a ton of weight had been lifted from him. The inner distress and guilt were replaced with peace. Anger seemed to be replaced with a new understanding of the faith of his wife. He felt a warm sense of exhilaration.

All of his life, J.A. Wilkerson did things in a big way and getting religion wasn't going to change his demonstrative nature. He just couldn't turn and walk out of that tent without letting God and the entire congregation knowing how he felt. Not my grandfather! He forgot about his weakened condition, forgot about his stiff leg, and let loose of all his past religious dignity. Suddenly, realizing he had experienced a miracle, he let out a yell and took off running. Around the tent he stormed, in and out of benches, as if he were chasing the devil that had so long been chasing him.

J.A. was a changed man and everyone knew it. Unashamedly, he felt the tears streaming down his face. Then remembering his diseased body, he stopped to tell God: "Lord, you can take me any time now. I'm ready to die."

Up until that night J.A. had fought to live, trying any remedy suggested to him. Each time J.A. had been for a medical checkup, both he and the doctor knew that the medication was having no effect either way. Now that he was ready to meet his maker, his only desire was to die. His tuberculosis had reached the last stages and there was no remedy of any kind left. The doctor had advised him to set his house in order and wait to die.

However, J.A. wasn't about to permit thoughts of death to overshadow his wonderful experience. He never doubted for one minute his change of mind and heart, although his friends publicly voiced their skepticism. They knew he had strayed far from his religious roots, and they weren't too sure that getting emotionally overwrought about saying the sinner's prayer really proved anything had happened to their friend. "It won't last," they predicted.

They were wrong.

Only Della believed that her husband would change. She had prepared in advance for the news of her husband's salvation. Within several days of receiving J.A.'s letter with the account of his transformation, she made arrangements to leave the children with church friends, and bought a train ticket for Danville. J.A., pleased Della had come, offered her his true repentance as a peace offering.

I wish I could say J.A.'s conversion brought about total happiness in their reunion, but it was difficult for them to hide their sadness from each other. Different religious views had divided them for a while, and the short separation had been painful, but they both knew that J.A.'s condition was serious, and they knew that the separation of death, which seemed imminent, would be forever.

At his next checkup, J.A. testified to the doctor of his conversion and then wistfully added: "You know, Doc, I wish God had healed my body as well as my soul. Some of those folks at the tent said He could, but I reckon that's asking God too much. At least I know now I'm ready to die."

J.A. shoved the bottles of medicine in his pocket and said to Della: "Let's go to the afternoon meeting. I could sure use some good preaching and singing."

His spirit needed a lift and he knew that a visit to the tent would give him much needed inspiration. He even dared to believe that God could heal. The evangelist made his plea for sinners to come forward and for the saints to gather round them. J.A. bowed his head to pray; he was too weak to join the others at the altar.

A soft voice spoke. "Brother Wilkerson, this is God's time to heal you." J.A. lifted his head and for a moment stared at the woman standing beside his bench; then, without hesitation he got up and obediently followed her to the altar. He laid the new bottle of medicine on the altar and the folks gathered around him; some put their hands on his head, others on his shoulders and then, with arms raised up to heaven, they commanded in Jesus' name that Satan loose his hold upon J.A.'s body. When their prayers subsided, the good sister leaned over and said, "Brother, you're healed now!" He hadn't felt a thing except the forcefulness and earnestness of the people's prayers. He stood up, whispered a hoarse, "Thank you," and he and Della went back to the boarding house—without the medication

No one at the meeting asked J.A. if he was healed. No one asked him to breathe deeply three times just to be sure. They prayed, they believed, and they pronounced him healed. When he left, they thanked God for answering their prayers.

God had indeed answered their prayers. With every step J.A. took toward the boardinghouse he could breathe a little more deeply. By the time they arrived at the steps, he could breathe normally. Together they ran up the steps and sat on the porch swing to give thanks for God's goodness.

Della rested her head on her husband's shoulder and whispered: "God really does perform miracles today."

J.A., being his usual exuberant self, shouted out a loud "Amen," but Della hadn't finished her thought. Looking J.A. in the eye, she quietly said: "Don't you think you need to give a public witness to your healing?"

The next morning, J.A. headed straight for the doctor's office. "Doc, I've been healed. Now, no one's going to believe me, not even you, so I want you to X-ray me again so I'll have proof." He didn't care what it would cost—he wanted proof to show the skeptics; he knew from personal experience that some would refuse to believe him without medical proof of his miracle.

The doctor already knew that his tuberculosis patient possessed a great deal of determination, so he agreed to J.A.'s request, wondering to himself how his patient would receive the news that nothing had happened. Needless to say, one look at the X-ray was enough proof for the doctor that God still performed miracles.

J.A. didn't need those X-rays to convince himself that God had healed him, but he planned to prove the authenticity of his testimony to the doubters. He would later preach about skeptics who set their minds against miracles, who refused to believe even if miracles happened before their eyes. He was sure his testimony would change the minds of the skeptics and pave the way for leading them to repent of their unbelief.

The night J.A. said the sinner's prayer, he had experienced another healing. It hadn't dawned upon him until he sat in the doctor's office that he had run around the tent like a crazy man without giving one thought to his stiff, aching leg. Without hesitation, he demonstrated his healing by swinging his leg over the doctor's chair. The doctor watched in amazement.

Both doctor and patient recognized that a miracle incomprehensible to the human mind had been preformed on J.A. God gave him a clean heart, healthy lungs, a healed stomach and renewed veins in his leg. Along with these miracles, God promised J.A. eternal life. He had positive proof of the operation by the Master Physician; he was a condemned man still alive!

"J.A.," the doctor enthusiastically responded, "you have my permission to tell people you experienced a miracle." Granddad told his story over and over, lifting his leg high over any piece of furniture that happened to be in his line of focus—including pulpits!

By now J.A. could look back and see the hand of the Lord humbling him to a place where he would realize his need for God. He wanted to make up for his stubbornness by giving himself to serving God. Remembering his past and the insult that he had shouted to the heavens, he now prayed: "Lord, if you still want me to preach the Gospel, I'm ready."

Danville seemed a good place to answer the call to preach and raise the children in the Nazarene church where Della and he attended. Della returned to Knoxville for Kenneth and Gertha while J.A. searched for a small apartment. He planned to settle in and find a place to preach—even if he had to start on the streets of the nearby communities. The zeal to tell his story of salvation and healing burned brightly in his heart—there would be no stopping J.A., he would be on the revival circuit for a long time.

## CHAPTER 4

# CHANGING PEWS

After J.A.'s healing, he began to envision how he would answer the call. He committed himself to anything the Lord wanted him to do and he intended to keep his promise. His propensity to take action on all the ideas racing through his mind had not changed. He immediately began making plans to show his gratitude to God and to tell the world that the God of the Apostles still preformed miracles of healing in the twentieth century.

My family's view about going out into the world to preach the Gospel is very simple. We take Christ's words literally: "Lift up your eyes, and look on the fields; for they are white already to harvest" (John 4:35 KJV). Neither prejudice nor politics kept our family from preaching the Gospel in fields all around us. Our example for such an unbiased religion was Granddad.

J.A. looked out and beheld the town of Westville with a population of about five hundred. Despite the cold and snow, he took off in a rented horse and buggy to save souls from the town's many saloons. With all his blustery exuberance, J.A. had a keen mind for details. He could tell you in sixty seconds flat how to get something done and how to get it done his way. He would plan his strategy and set out for the attack.

Westville's drunkards were too dazed and too busy huddling around potbelly stoves trying to keep warm in the bitter winter to notice strange noises above one of their hangouts. J.A. and Brother Bill, a friend from the church where Della and he had joined, cleaned out an old storeroom, installed a coal stove for heat, hung oil lamps, and then stretched out wooden planks among a dozen or so "sanctified" beer kegs for the pews.

For several weekends, J.A. and Brother Bill faithfully trotted the old horse and buggy stacked with kindling wood to their harvest field. They lighted the stove and lamps and then warmed themselves on their knees in prayer. The homemade sign in the window read, EVERYONE WELCOME, but no one took the bait. Night after night, J.A.'s banjo filled the room with the old-time religion songs. They prayed loud enough to be heard above the noise below them. They formed "Jericho marches" around the beer kegs claiming at least one soul within the sound of their voices. Then they stopped to listen, not a footstep was heard.

When J.A. instituted a program, it never failed because it was planned provisionally, and subject to change the minute it needed revamping. "Brother Bill," he announced to his friend on the second night, "it's time we put feet to our prayers." They trudged from door to door through the winter snow hoping for a warm welcome from anyone at all.

It takes a stranger in foreign surroundings to recognize another in a similar situation. Joe Debarber and his family were so happy to have two kindly and sober gentlemen drop by for a visit that they threw open the door inviting the strangers to warm themselves at their kitchen stove.

J.A.sat near the potbelly stove to warm his numbed hands, then with a big smile leaned back and proceeded to rattle off his exciting testimony. Eight pairs of dark eyes stared, their heads nodding. "Yah, yah," they responded, pretending to understand their fast-talking visitor, who talked so well in the language they were trying to master.

Suddenly recognizing the language barrier, J.A. realized he would have to improvise with his own sign language or depend on God to get the message across. He slowly enunciated the words: "Will you let me pray for you?"

Ah, prayer Joe knew. Many, many times the family had prayed to the saints and to Mary. "Yah, Yah, you pray."

J.A. prayed as only he knew how—loud and fervently—for

all the family to believe in Christ as their Savior. They stared in amazement. "Oh, oh! Dis man, he wake Papa," whispered Mama Debarber.

Sure enough, out walked Grandpa Debarber in his nightshirt, spilling out words unrepeatable in any language. J.A. flashed his big smile, invited them to attend the revival services, and made haste to leave.

The next evening, J.A. and his faithful partner began the service as usual, their ears alert for the sounds of footsteps. J.A. felt something in his bones. Soon he heard the sound of heavy footsteps. In silence they stared at the door. Very slowly it opened, and there stood Mr. Debarber.

For the benefit of their congregation they started the service over. They sang, they prayed, and J.A. preached—only this time, he made his message plain. It was of the utmost importance for Mr. Debarber to understand that he must come to the altar to pray the sinner's prayer.

At long last, the light of truth dawned upon his soul and he haltingly prayed the sinner's prayer. Had it not been for the instant joy mirrored on their convert's face, they would have thought the sinner only admitted guilt to escape their clutches. Further proof of Mr. Debarber's conversion came the next night when eight more people sat on the pews and attentively listened while J.A. worked up a sweat trying to explain the Gospel to rest of the family.

Back home, J.A. told the story of his first revival over and over to Della. He had his first taste of preaching, and it was good. He planned to establish a church in the community and hoped Della would make the four-mile trolley trip to teach the women's Bible classes and conduct prayer meetings in Westville.

By then, J.A. had joined the Pentecostal Nazarene Church in which he had been saved. Because he had a hunger to know the Scriptures and did not appreciate younger preachers knowing more than he did, he took the advice of his mentors and entered the Olivet University of the Nazarene Church. With a keen ability to retain almost everything he heard or read, he began a diligent campaign to memorize the Scriptures. At the time he joined this denomination, the name "Pentecostal" was attached, but, around this time, a great controversy arose about the experience in the Book of Acts of the baptism of the Holy Spirit with speaking in unknown languages. When these "tongues-speaking" people joined together to organize a fellowship, the Nazarene church wanted the world to know that they were not part of the fellowship and wanted nothing to do with speaking in unknown tongues. They voted to drop the name Pentecostal.

J.A., still a "babe in Christ" but not young in years, decided he would not allow a body of men to decide for him what was or wasn't of God. He searched the Scriptures and approached his teacher, Sister Serena Jay, with the argument that if the Apostles needed to be baptized by the Holy Spirit to preach the Gospel, certainly he needed this same power to help convert the world.

Sister Jay was quick to warn J.A. to be careful. "Much fanaticism is sweeping the country; you must not get involved with this false doctrine. Forget about it and learn the deeper things of God, such as sanctification." He regarded the words of his godly teacher with respect, temporarily putting this part of the Scriptures from his mind, but thinking to himself, "Some day, God will show me the meaning of this New Testament experience."

His zeal and eagerness to learn made J.A. a good preacher and he gained a reputation for being cooperative with his brethren. The word started to spread about J.A. Wilkerson: "Let this man preach for you and the people will come running to the altars."

In 1913, J.A. was elected as the Chicago Central District Evangelist and served in this capacity for two years. J.A. began a tour to conduct revivals in tents during the summer months and in churches in the colder months. Friends from the Danville church volunteered to keep the children in their homes so that

Della could travel with her husband. J.A. depended on her to lead the women's prayer meetings and to take care of his needs. Shirts had to be mended, starched, and ironed; suits had to be pressed and shoes shined. J.A. had never learned to cope with earthly matters.

One eventful evening during a tent revival conducted near Olivet University, J.A. and his band of ministerial students came face to face with a group of Pentecostals who had come to hear the well-known evangelist. They came with their songbooks and Bibles tucked under their arms, their faces beaming with the excitement of their recent spiritual experience. The appearance of these "fanatics" caused a good deal of anxiety among the students. All during the song service they kept their heads bowed, praying in a low murmur to rebuke the devils in their midst. The students' agitation became all the more apparent when they noticed the evangelist warming up to the visitors who sang with vigor and loudly voiced their amens.

One of the young students dared to step forward and warn J.A.: "Don't let these devils get hold of our service. They're bound to scare the rest of the folks away." J.A. hadn't seen any devils. The Pentecostals had stayed in their seats just like any other visitors.

"You let that be my worry. I know how to handle devils!" Calmly he listened to the testimonies, trying to ignore the angry sounds behind him. It didn't take long to discern which group exhibited the Spirit of Christ. After that service, not one student would attend J.A.'s revival services. The tent was taken down and J.A. knew it was time to move on.

Not long after this encounter, J.A. felt he was meant to go back to his hometown of Knoxville. Since J.A. depended on Della to take care of his needs and to assist him in the evangelistic revivals, they decided to place Gertha and Kenneth in the Wesleyan Methodist boarding school in Greenville, South Carolina. They sincerely believed God required their full attention to preaching the Gospel, and so they willingly made the sacrifice of parting with the children, not realizing the devastating affect their decision would have upon them.

J.A. had a successful evangelistic ministry all through the South, beginning with the Patton Street Church and the Beaumont Wesleyan Methodist Church in Knoxville. The meetings often lasted four to six weeks, with people faithfully attending each night and bringing their unsaved friends and relatives. Della worked alongside her husband teaching women in afternoon sessions and leading ladies' prayer meetings.

The revival meetings were oftentimes met with vehement opposition. J.A. did two controversial things—he welcomed the "coloreds" to his tent revivals and he was known for confronting sinners and unashamedly spelling out the sin question. He said he didn't give a hoot what the "whites" thought or that a town depended on tobacco and corn to keep them prospering. He still welcomed anyone who wanted to come to his meetings and stormed the platform, marching up and down the aisles and shaking his fist at the devil, declaring that smokers and drinkers were defiling the temple of the Lord and that the wages of their sin was hell.

In Loudon, Tennessee, he stirred up a hornet's nest. He dared to preach right at the members of the Odd Fellows who were sitting in the congregation and gave away some of the lodge secrets, which he felt were contrary to the Scriptures. The fury that shook the lodge members exploded into a plan to kill the evangelist. The local blacksmith gladly volunteered to do the job, vowing that he would not let that "damnable preacher" out of town alive. Word spread as fast as a brush fire from house to house.

Tension ran high that night. The church was packed. There were faces peering in every window and guns in every corner. The only calm one among them was J.A. He stood up to preach, closing his eyes to ask God to bless the Word. Before he could address God, a rustle of feet interrupted the silence. Grandma Ruby, an elderly member feared and respected for her stand against sin, jumped to her feet and headed down the aisle, her eyes blazing with a righteous fury. Unafraid, she faced the congregation, speaking loudly for all to hear: "This preacher knows God and I know Loudon. The first man who lays a hand on him will get this," and she pulled an eighteen inch butcher knife from under her apron and held it high for all the men to see.

She sat down in the front pew while J.A. preached a stirring message. "It was, by far, the best night of the campaign. Many souls were saved, many bodies healed and the faith of the congregation increased because of their victory over the enemy of their souls," recalled J.A. when he told the story of Grandma Ruby's bravery.

The Odd Fellows met to make new plans, but one of the members stood up and said, "Brothers, my wife's attending that meeting and I'm not going to lay a hand on one soul up there."

Another man stood and said, "My mother attends them services and I ain't having nothing to do with this either."

They could not come to an agreement as to how to get rid of the evangelist, so they adjourned. Their plot was defeated.

J.A. attracted people to his meetings by testifying about what the Lord had done for him. He walked through "colored" neighborhoods and the downtown streets going in and out of stores, saloons and offices of town magistrates and pinned them down, one by one, to promising to attend church that very night. If they weren't there, they'd be sure to get a second invitation. If there still was no response and J.A. felt a burden for a particular person, he would ask people to pray until the sinner repented. And then if the rebellious one would not listen to his pleading, he'd say, "I'm shaking the dust off my feet. Hell will be ten times hotter for you now!"

J.A. and Della spent two successful years traveling in

Tennessee and the surrounding states. Few revival meetings took them to South Carolina to visit their children, and Della's letters weren't much comfort to ease their loneliness. During the two lonely years at the boarding school, Gertha, the older of the two, took it upon herself to mother her little brother. Even so, little Kenneth cried his heart out every night, wanting to be with his mother. Bravely, they both endured school until finally Kenneth, lonely and heartbroken, grew listless, not wanting to eat or play. No one could console him. "My brother's just homesick," Gertha told the doctor who examined him.

Gertha decided to end their distress once and for all. She took all the money she had saved up, left the school without a word and bought a train ticket. Gertha, with her father's boldness and her mother's spirited determination to right the wrongs, planned to convince her parents they were neglecting their children.

J.A. and Della were leading a revival service near Knoxville, Tennessee, when the sudden appearance of their thirteen-year-old daughter brought the meeting to a halt. Needless to say, her mother and father stood dumbfounded when they saw Gertha walk into the service. Her plan had worked! The children were never again sent to live separately from the family.

J.A. rented a home in Knoxville and went out alone to preach. During World War I, he no longer received sufficient offerings to support the family. He applied for work at the trolley company again, but they went on strike. Waiting out the weeks for a settlement, he found himself involved in an unusual ministry because of the flu epidemic, which eventually affected almost every family. J.A. traveled side by side with Dr. West, the physician who had once told him there was no hope for his recovery, on his rounds to the sick. "Dr. West fed people pills and I fed them Gos-pills," said Granddad.

Since no settlement of the strike seemed in view, J.A. decided to go to Ohio to find work with the northern subsidiary of the traction company. The family stayed behind until sufficient money could be saved for their fares to Ohio.

The old files of the Northern Ohio Traction Company contain newspaper stories that tell of a strike that was settled by one of the workers who also was an evangelist. It seems J.A. wasn't going to sit down and take the strike of his company lightly—he had a family to support. He had worked with the men of the company for four years, he knew the cause of the strike and he knew a few hidden secrets of some of the bosses.

J.A. went into action with one of his "programs." Straight to the president he went. "Mr. Scanlon, I believe I can help settle this strike. Just give me a chance to preach to these men on Sunday afternoons in the trolley barn and you'll see a miracle." Mr. Scanlon was skeptical, but being a devout Catholic, he hoped the spiritual influence might do the men some good, so he granted J.A. permission.

J.A. entered the barn on the following Sunday, took off his shoes, jumped up on the large table called the mahogany and started preaching to the men who were gathered in small groups around the tables, gambling. One by one, men put down their cards. Some listened, some scoffed, but J.A. shouted above the complaints. "Some of you men have stolen from this company, most of you cheat on the time and work you give the company, and yet you sit around expecting the management to give you better hours and better pay. What you really need are clean hands and clean hearts."

A few Sundays of old-time religion began to hit the mark. When it came time for the next meeting of the leaders to settle on the contract, they gladly signed. The strike had ended. The president called J.A. into his office, "Reverend Wilkerson, this strike has been settled by your preaching. Now I want to know what I can do for you."

I guess J.A. could have had just about any position in the company at that time. But he had his mind on only one goal: to win more men to the Lord. His call came before himself and his family. "Mr. Scanlon, all I want is permission for the barn to be my church every Sunday." Mr. Scanlon gladly obliged. Each Sunday the tables were moved aside, seats were set up and J.A. stood on the mahogany to preach. Many men were converted and out of that group two made a decision to preach the Gospel.

Around that time, J.A. had a new spiritual experience that would greatly impact his ministry. He had met Charles McKinney, a preacher at the Pentecostal Assemblies of God Church in Akron, Ohio. Charles told J.A. he needed to receive the baptism of the Holy Spirit. When he learned the experience would give him special power to preach the Gospel, he made up his mind to receive this baptism evidenced in the life of his new friend.

Soon after their conversation, J.A. received an invitation to preach in his nephew's church in Alcoa, Tennessee. It was in this Church of God revival that J.A. experienced the power of the Holy Spirit upon him in the middle of his sermon. J.A. would later tell Della that he thought for sure he was being translated into heaven. He had, at last, experienced the power and mystery of the Holy Spirit that he had wondered about for so long.

When he got back to Akron, J.A. shared his new spiritual experience with Della, and they searched for a Church of God. There happened to be a little chapel on Massillon Road with a congregation that had been praying for God to send along a pastor. The night J.A. dropped in for a visit, they found their pastor.

Then without warning, tragedy suddenly struck the family. Della had seldom been sick. So when she became ill, neither she nor J.A. found her loss of strength to be alarming. "It's just this toothache that is bothering me," she said. But the infection was much worse than they thought and by the time it was diagnosed, it was too late to stop the blood poisoning in her body. Della died on October 22, 1922.

Even though Gertha was eighteen, and Kenneth sixteen, J.A. did not know how to keep the family together. It had been Della's love and prayers that had guided J.A. and the children through rough times. They grieved alone together; there was no family nearby to share in their grief. J.A. had no one to console him. He had lost his best friend and his ministry partner.

J.A. had accepted the position of District Overseer along with the Massillon Road pastorate and felt it impossible, with his busy schedule, to keep a house. He sold most of the furnishings and moved the family into a small apartment. Church activities eased J.A.'s loss. He continued pouring his life into his pastoral and evangelistic responsibilities. His absences caused the children's grief to deepen. Even though they were both older, it seemed as if they were being abandoned all over again.

In February, J.A. received a call to conduct a revival from the Church of God in Fostoria. When he visited the church, the beautiful young woman who served the Lord playing the piano for the church, caught J.A.'s attention. He took one look at lovely Maxine and told the pastor, "I intend to marry your pianist." Maxine was nineteen years old—J.A. was forty.

J.A. married his second wife on March 15, 1923, in Toledo, Ohio. Reverend Rembert, the Ohio state overseer of the Church of God, performed their marriage ceremony. Though he would always remember Della, J.A. was no longer lonely and he was pleased to find a talented wife to help him in the work of the Lord. He was of the opinion that all preachers of the Gospel needed a good wife to keep them living a moral life.

But for the two children who needed a mother and father to help them in their teenage years, their father's marriage to a woman just a year older than Gertha gave them reason to believe they could no longer be a family. Gertha decided she would not wait to marry the young man to whom she was engaged, but she worried about her brother. She had promised her mother she would watch over him.

It was J.A. who made the decision about sixteen-year-old Kenneth. Since the two-room apartment left no place for children, he boarded his son Kenneth in the home of a parishioner. This sudden uprooting became a source of contention between father and son. Kenneth determined to part with his father and make his own way in life.

After his new marriage, J.A. kept his pastorate and position as District Overseer for two years; then he received a call to be pastor in Cleveland, Tennessee. During his time there, he came into sharp disagreement with the policies of the denomination and decided to break with the Church of God and enter the Pentecostal fellowship of his good friend, Pastor McKinney.

His first pastorate with the Assemblies of God was in Hammond, Indiana. J.A. took a small congregation, put a strong spiritual program to work, and built up the church to one of the denomination's finest.

Just as in his revivals, he met with much opposition because of his unconventional ways, but J.A. had a way with people and they had to like him in spite of his theatrical antics. Many converts joined the church and some of them were inspired to enter full-time ministry because of the story of J.A.'s call to preach.

CHAPTER 5

# THE SON CLAIMS HIS INHERITANCE

At the age of sixteen, Kenneth left home without any thought of claiming the only inheritance his father could give him. The memory of a praying mother and the testimony of his father's healing seemed of little value to sustain his faith in an unbelieving and hostile world. Although their relationship was strained, a serious father-son discussion resulted in the conclusion that Kenneth still needed adult guidance. The best plan seemed to be to take advantage of one of Uncle Sam's opportunities for service to the country.

Kenneth chose the Marines. He found that it immediately satisfied all his needs for that particular time of his life. Besides a good place to sleep and the surety of three meals a day, he found comfort in the daily routine of military life, and took pride parading in his always immaculate uniform. Opportunities to meet people and have new cultural experiences eased his homesickness. Adhering to rigid rules gave him a sense of accomplishment and security. Years later, Dad would tell us that he could read a man's character by the way he respected the laws of God and government and by the neatness of his clothes and the shine of his shoes.

Kenneth entered into his new phase of life with more zeal

than it seemed a minister's son should possess. Deliberately, he chose the paths of sin that would completely disengage him from any connection to the Pentecostals. Suddenly he had become a man, and he intended to prove himself as much a man-of-the-world as any other Marine.

Fearful that his holiness connection would be discovered, Kenneth immediately informed his buddies that he was the son of a Methodist minister. Since no reproach seemed attached to membership in a well-known and respected church, he felt free to be like one of the boys.

His willful ways proved to be his downfall and revealed him to his buddies for what he really was: a young fellow packed so full of holiness preaching that it had to come out sometime. It seems an unusual phenomenon occurred when he had a couple of drinks. By nature, he was serious and intense about life, but give him two drinks and his personality became transformed from that of a sedate Methodist layman to a hell-fire and brimstone preacher. Unfortunately, the episodic preaching could only be manifested under intoxicated conditions, so his preaching had little effect on his "spirited" congregation.

Kenneth's first enlistment, spent mostly on duty in Florida, Haiti and the St. Thomas Islands, changed him from a bewildered, naive boy to a confident, well-trained and dependable young man. At the end of his four years, he felt prepared to face the work force again, but when he went back to Akron to visit his sister, he found himself right back where he had started four years earlier. Nothing had changed.

He was still without a home, although his sister and her husband readily opened their home to him. To make matters worse, during his military years he had never saved for a rainy day and now he was penniless. So there he sat, literally without a cent, unskilled and much too proud to borrow from his sister. There seemed to be no jobs available for former Marines.

It seemed natural to Kenneth to return to the only life he

knew for his career. Rejoining the Marines for a second enlistment gave him a higher rank. Now a Sergeant, he requested the job of recruiting officer and was stationed in Cleveland, Ohio.

Recruiting men for the Marines was a surprisingly difficult assignment. Eight hours of the day he stood at a small booth located in Cleveland's Public Square. It was his job to talk men into joining the Marines rather than the Army or the Navy and it called for some fancy talking. Kenneth had his mother's authoritative demeanor and a dash of his father's gift of persuasive oratory. He and his buddy took turns sizing up a fellow. They devised a unique system—one of them would tell a joke and while the prospect let out with a hearty laugh, the other Marine checked the candidate's teeth. A good set of teeth was a must for the Marines.

On his free time, Kenneth and his friend frequented most of Cleveland's dance halls. His rebellious smoking and drinking that sometimes led to brawls bothered Kenneth's conscience, but dancing was different. He enjoyed dancing and preferred the dance halls to the bars. In every port he managed to win trophies for doing a flawless Charleston. In spite of tired feet, he always fared as well on the dance floor as he did on the job, especially one spring night in 1928.

Standing just inside a dance hall, he searched the floor, sizing up the girls, looking for the prettiest and the best dancer. When he spotted a lovely blond with a beautiful smile flitting around in the arms of another man, he boldly cut in, taking into his arms a girl he described as "five-foot two, eyes of blue." He had found a perfect dancing partner.

Before the evening was over, he had decided that this beautiful blond was the girl for him, but Ann Marton, already engaged for two years, wasn't so easily convinced. The only information she offered him was the address of where she worked. She had no intention of falling for a stranger who had brazenly assumed she would agree to a sudden proposal. After all, she was a modern girl, enjoying the freedom of working and making her own decisions.

The next morning, Kenneth surprised the pretty secretary by meeting her as she got off the streetcar at Public Square. "Well, Sergeant, you don't waste time, do you!" Sensing no rebuff and no refusal to meet him at the dance hall, he determined to keep pressuring Ann for an answer. Kenneth, much like his father, wasted no time in perusing things he wanted. But it took him three months to convince Ann that she should call off her engagement and marry him. They were married on July 29, 1928.

Although Kenneth was tall and handsome, and Ann thought that he was a Methodist, she did not marry him for his good looks or his religious background. Ann had been raised in a religious home; her parents were Lutherans who made sure their children studied catechism. Ann had a better knowledge of the Bible than Kenneth, but she had never understood that Christians could have a close relationship with God. Her prayers were limited to a few written ones she had either memorized or read from a prayer book.

When Ann met Kenneth her interests were strictly worldly. If you asked her if she was a Christian, she'd quickly answer, "Of course, my name is on the rolls of the Lutheran church, and I usually attend on Sunday." But her desires for the "things of the world" began early in her teenage years. She became fascinated with the new dress styles and music of the roaring twenties. When her parents could no longer control her cravings for the latest fads, they sent her to Cleveland to live with an uncle to attend a Lutheran school. Living away from the restriction of parents only sparked a greater interest in the latest fashions and swing music. Dancing became her passion—every night she visited a dance hall with her friends—competing for the greatest number of dances for the evening.

Because she had met Kenneth at a dance hall, and he seemed a man of the world, Ann assumed he would fit into her life style.

She also knew that her parents would be delighted she was marrying a Methodist minister's son. She hoped it would make amends for the grief she had caused them. She couldn't wait to take him to Pennsylvania to meet her family in Canonsburg.

When it came to choosing which church they would attend, Ann suggested that they attend her church. Kenneth stubbornly refused and the issue became their first source of disagreement.

"Then I'll attend the Methodist church with you," Ann offered, wanting to start their marriage in agreement about religion. Much to her consternation, her husband even refused to attend his own church. A few arguments ensued, often taking place around the table of friends living in the apartment below.

"I don't want to attend your church, Ann, and I don't want to attend the Methodist church!" Kenneth was adamant. Ann couldn't understand what was so wrong with the Lutherans.

"And just what is wrong with my church?" she demanded to know.

"Well, Ann, if you want to know, your church is dead!"

Ann laughed. She was inclined to agree, but she knew no other church. "Well, my dear husband, at least you can't say we act like the Holy Rollers." She wasn't sure how they did act, but she had heard they danced and shouted, even going so far as to roll on the floors.

Kenneth pushed back his chair, his eyes blazing. "What do you mean by that remark, Ann? Are you calling me a Holy Roller?"

"Why, Kenneth, why are you so angry? Why should I call you a Holy Roller? I don't even know what they are; anyway, you can't say Methodists are Holy Rollers!" Ann simply could not understand her husband's strong reaction.

Kenneth checked his anger. A confession lingered at the tip of his tongue; it had been there since the day he married. Now he worried if he would ever find the right moment to reveal that his religion was often called the Holy Roller Church. Mother eyed Dad with suspicion. She was certain that there was a reason for his anger.

Kenneth kept putting off the day of confession and fortunately for him, he wasn't around when Ann solved the mystery of her husband's angry outburst. They had been married only a few months when orders were given for the Cleveland recruiting office to close up and send its men to report for duty at Quantico, Virginia. Ann was expecting their first child and since Kenneth did not want to leave her alone while he settled into a new post, they accepted his father's offer for her to live with them at the Hammond, Indiana church parsonage.

Kenneth had married without asking permission of the Marines. His father advised him to set things straight and ask to be relieved of duty to take up a career more suitable for raising a family. Permission to marry was denied, so Kenneth decided to tell the truth—still the Marines would not honor his request.

"Son, you go on to Virginia. My church will pray. God will get your life set in order." Kenneth went back to the Marines and Ann went to Hammond to live in the parsonage.

Ann felt welcomed by the Wilkerson household, but she sensed something that she could not identify. She had put her best foot forward, carefully attiring herself in her most modest clothes (which weren't modest enough, according to holiness traditions). She even toned down her makeup, but there wasn't much she could do about her short, bobbed hair.

On the weekend, she dutifully announced that she would attend their church services. Sunday morning they drove up to a large barn-like building. At first glance, Ann was sure it was not a Methodist church, but on closer inspection, the inside appeared to be a sanctuary. She was pleasantly surprised to see a large crowd, which spoke well for her father-in-law. Then, as newcomers are naturally prone to do, Ann began to look at the people. Several strange peculiarities were quite evident. She realized at once that she was not modestly dressed. Her makeup, even the style of her hair, looked different than the other women in the church.

And she could not help but notice that people had their arms raised up and everyone prayed out loud during the congregational prayers and spontaneously, without the aid of a prayer book. Most alarming for Ann were people praying in a strange language rather than in English. "Why, these people are crazy!" she thought to herself. It did not take long before she realized what Kenneth had been trying to hide—he was the son of a Holy Roller preacher and she, a staunch Lutheran, was sitting in a holiness church service!

She was furious, even seething, over her husband's deception. "How will I ever get out of this? And just you wait, Kenneth. You have some answering to do for me," she murmured under her breath. She began plotting ways to escape the embarrassment of being connected with the Holy Rollers.

J.A. had anticipated the reaction of his daughter-in-law. Careful not to add fuel to her inward fire, he allowed Ann time to decide for herself what to do with her discovery. They warmly welcomed her into their home and the church, all the while going about the Lord's work, and never once explained or apologized for their peculiar behavior.

Ann left the service that morning declaring that she would never go back again and get mixed up with such an odd group. Unknown to Ann, J.A. had already given a request for her enlightenment to the ladies' prayer meeting. Son Kenneth was included in those prayers. Now it was "Operation Children" in the Hammond church.

J.A. did let Ann know that they were praying for Kenneth to be released from the Marines. She believed in prayer and she graciously thanked her in-laws, but she was more pleased about the prospects of her husband rescuing her out of the holiness surroundings.

It seemed to her that the Wilkerson family lived more at

church than at home. Prayer meetings and Bible studies filled each morning, afternoons were spent visiting parishioners, and evangelistic rallies were held several nights a week. For a while, she viewed the routine with disdain. But gradually her animosity lessened—she was being won over by their love and acceptance of her worldly ways. Slowly, the prayers of the women began to take effect. Like spring gradually blossoming forth, Ann's interest to know more about God grew. Emerging from her anger and pride, she made her second announcement: "I'm going to your church this Sunday." Curiosity had gotten the best of her. She had to go back once more.

This time the people didn't appear to be crazy. This time the spirit of the services reached deep inside, plucking a chord of spiritual hunger held so long within. During the congregational prayers, Ann raised her hand before God. Words of thanksgiving and praise tumbled out of her mouth; she could not stop the flow of adoration to the Lord. Tears ran freely as she voiced her love for the Lord—it seemed as if the presence of God had filled the sanctuary and she sensed His nearness. She wondered: "Is this what it means to be on holy ground?"

She felt no embarrassment; it suddenly seemed very natural to worship God from her heart and with her lips. For the first time, she found Christianity a joyous and satisfying faith. She wanted to tell everyone what God had done for her, and she especially wanted her husband to know.

"Honey," she wrote, "I've been really, truly changed." Kenneth couldn't believe it. What had they done to get his worldly wife to become a spiritual woman? And what about her love for the things of the world? What would she do when she discovered his father's church listed almost all the things she cared about as sin? He would have to see it to believe it!

Now the congregation began an earnest plea for Kenneth's release from the Marines. To his amazement, orders for his release were granted. Soon he was on a train speeding through several states to Indiana. The long trip gave him time to rehearse excuses for not admitting to Ann that he was a son of a Pentecostal preacher. All the while, the clicking of the wheels penetrated his troubled conscience. He was startled to hear himself putting words to the click, click, click of the train wheels: "I'm going to get saved. I'm going to get saved." The thought repeated over and over with increasing intensity.

By the time the train had pulled into the Hammond station, he had made up his mind: no more drinking or smoking, and he would even give up his favorite pleasure—dancing the Charleston. He wanted to start a new life free of guilt and shame; he wanted to give his life to Christ. If Ann could change, he would too.

He arrived home, giving no hint of his decision to accept the faith of his father and now, also the faith of his wife. It wasn't until he attended church and boldly stepped forward to the altar that the entire church knew their prayers had been answered. That very night, Granddad added step two to his plan for his son. He hoped to train his son in what he had neglected to teach him during his teenage years and intended to see that he was thoroughly grounded in the Scriptures.

## CHAPTER 6

# IN HIS FATHER'S FOOTSTEPS

J.A. had no qualms about his son's future. He believed, that with his help, his firstborn son would follow in his footsteps. With that thought, J.A. launched Kenneth into a study of the Bible and of his own unique philosophy on pastoral theology. Each day, he shadowed his father through ministerial duties; sometimes he was asked to pray for a parishioner on their visitation rounds, or give his testimony to strangers whom J.A. might stop on the street, or teach a beginner's Bible class, and occasionally, J.A. yielded his pulpit to find out if his son was grasping the teachings of the Bible.

Ann watched her husband's training process for several weeks with mounting annoyance, until one day she spoke her mind: "Kenneth, we can't keep living off your father. There's not enough room for us here. I think we should find our own place to live and have a steady income." Ann had a concern for a steady income as much as having privacy. Living with family and a life of poverty seemed to be exactly where they were heading if her husband didn't soon find a salaried job, and it didn't set well with her.

Kenneth, by this time, had totally involved himself in the activities of the church and it took every bit of his time. This is how he liked it. It became spiritual "meat and drink" to him, but his earthly duties called. He had no intention of being a burden to his father or letting his own family suffer, so without a word to anyone, he began the search for a job. One day, he arrived home tired but pleased to announce to his wife: "Ann, I've got a job! And you'll never guess how much I'll make—fifteen dollars a week! Imagine that!"

Ann could barely contain her joy. Now they could move into their own apartment, and clothes given to her by well-meaning church members could now be discarded. To add to her joy, baby Juanita arrived. It seemed she had every thing to make her happy. She was even finding a deep satisfaction in her husband's Pentecostal religion.

At a young age, Ann had learned Bible history and had memorized many answers to the catechism questions, but she had never understood how to apply the Scriptures to her life. Now she was sitting under J.A.'s teaching and he excelled in teaching his version of applied Christianity with a strong holiness slant that consisted of many rules and regulations to please God and man.

Since Ann had a sincere desire to achieve true holiness, she felt she had to follow explicitly the teachings of her father-in-law. If he said it was wrong to wear feathers, she ripped them from her hats. When he preached against jewelry, she guiltily eyed her wedding ring. The more J.A. preached against it, and the more she saw others placing jewelry on the altar, the more the ring bothered her. Finally, she could not stand to wear the ring on her finger any longer. Without a word to her husband she mailed the ring back to Cleveland, shocking not only Kenneth, but the jeweler, too.

After a few months of holiness indoctrination, Ann was definitely not the same worldly woman who had arrived looking like a modern day Jezebel (as she would later described herself), and her change found favor with her relatives and with the church members.

Ann's greatest change took place in her own home: she obeyed Christ's instruction to find a secret closet of prayer. In those early stages of learning to pray, Ann could not foresee how she was being prepared for a role she could never have imagined. There were times in her life when she faltered over strict holiness teachings; nevertheless, in those first years of her Christian growth, she established a love for God and faith in the trustworthiness of God that sustained us all—and still does even though she is gone.

Kenneth's Christian walk showed maturity and after rigorous months of training, he approached his father about trying out his preaching wings. J.A. lined up a few speaking engagements in several small churches with the instructions: "Now, Son, know what you're going to say, back it up with Scripture and give it to them with both barrels." That's the way J.A. did it, and he thrust his newborn preacher out, expecting his message to inspire people to new spiritual heights.

His sermon descended with a thud, but he did make one important discovery on his first solo flight in the pulpit—he was not the shadow of his father. He had inherited a few characteristics of father—he could hold his audiences spellbound to the Word—but he couldn't exhibit J.A.'s style. All attempts to be like his father ended in disaster, he lacked his father's sense of the dramatic, and knew he would never preach or pastor in the style of his father.

J.A. issued an ultimatum: "Son, you aren't ready to go out on your own. You need more training and more than I can give you." And he told his son the vision God had given him. "I saw a barge loaded with fruits and vegetables in the middle of the riverbed, but there wasn't a drop of water and the barge couldn't move. Son, I believe God has a ministry for you, but you are like that barge—you lack the water of the Holy Spirit to get it moving."

Several weeks after J.A.'s vision, Dr. Miller of Peniel Bible School in Dayton, Ohio, came to the Hammond church to conduct a series of Bible studies. Of course, J.A. told Dr. Miller about his son Kenneth and his need for Bible training. The good

Professor listened and watched. He sensed potential in Kenneth and approached him with an offer that changed the course of his life. "Kenneth, if you'll come to Peniel, I'll personally get you a scholarship that will take care of all your expenses."

Kenneth and J.A. were positive that God had answered their prayers, but Ann was concerned. "How can you go off and leave us here, expecting your father to support us, especially with our second baby coming?" With his father so certain and his wife in tears, Kenneth stood at the crossroads of a decision that would shape the destiny of his entire family.

Could it be that his mother's prayers were still in effect? It must have been so. He made the decision. "Honey, I feel the call of God. You must understand this; I am not forsaking you and the baby. If you're going to be a minister's wife, you must learn to trust God. Something will work out."

Words of promise were not enough for Ann. "I can't understand why God would separate us. Why would He join us together, and then suddenly take us apart? I don't believe God works this way." She stubbornly stuck to her logic.

Fortunately, Ann had been quick to believe in one of the strongest Pentecostal teachings: God honors the prayer of faith. She went to her prayer closet and to the ladies' prayer group. "Sisters," she pleaded her cause, "you must help me pray. If Kenneth goes to school then I must go, too." The sympathetic women took to their knees; they were going to pray until help came through from heaven for Sister Ann. They called this "praying through" until the answer came.

They made preparations for the move: Ann and Juanita to the Wilkerson's and Kenneth to Dayton, Ohio. The departure day loomed like a day of disaster and still there was no answer to their dilemma. Good-byes were said and Kenneth left without the family.

Two weeks later, Ann attended an all-day rally in Chicago with a delegation of women from the Hammond church. During the activities of the day, she met Mrs. Fleming Van Meter, wife of the State Superintendent of the Assemblies of God. The gracious lady gave Ann a warm Christian welcome to her husband's district and before she knew what was happening, Ann was sobbing out her story. The old adage, "Tell it to a woman and it will get done," must be true. The power of the prayers of the church sisters delivered Ann to the very person who could help. She wasn't sure what went on between Mr. and Mrs. Van Meter, but soon after the services in Chicago, she received a call from the Bible School.

The call came from the school's registrar, but for Ann it was a message from heaven: "Would you like to take an office position here at the school? We understand you would like to join your husband. This job would more than meet your expenses." In less than a week, the family was reunited and living in one room of the couple's dormitory.

Kenneth attended school for only one year, but it gave him a firm foundation on which he continued to build throughout his ministry. To the Bible classes, he added Bible courses from correspondence schools and hours of his own research through the Scriptures.

When school ended in May, 1931, Kenneth and his family arrived at the Hammond parsonage just in time to take part in a conspiracy to hide three of J.A. and Maxine's children, who were sprinkled with measles, from the family doctor who had made a house call to deliver Maxine's fourth child. J.A.'s holiness standard did not include obeying the quarantine laws of the State of Indiana; he believed a higher law required his presence in the home and in the church. In the midst of nursing sick children, Ann had to be hustled off to bed—baby number two was due any time.

J.A. hired two nurses: one for duty downstairs with the children and another with the mothers on the second floor. Maxine had a baby girl and named her Mary Ann, and Ann had a ten-pound baby boy and named him David, praying that her son would be like King David, killing many giants for the Lord. The children recovered from the measles without being discovered by the doctor and soon the parsonage was alive with children running, laughing, and crying. Maxine seemed oblivious to the noisy household, but Ann longed for privacy.

While Kenneth did his best to make it easier for Ann, his father mapped out his son's future. The nearby community of Indiana Harbor lacked a Pentecostal church and J.A. took it upon himself to see that a mission was established in this town of steel mills. What better prospective pastor was there than his own son to establish a new congregation?

Kenneth eagerly joined in the plans, his enthusiasm overriding feelings of apprehension. His father's assistance and the wholehearted cooperation of the church soothed his doubts.

Going from house to house, they worked hard to encourage people to visit the new church. Each night, services were conducted to attract people from the community to the new church. When one method failed, they came up with another, but it seemed that the venture had been doomed from the very beginning. The town wasn't interested in a Pentecostal church no matter what they had to offer. Kenneth marked the episode a failure he did not want to repeat and gave his thoughts to charting another course.

The failure shook his confidence. He felt he had failed his father, the church, his family, and worse yet, failed God. Talking, thinking and planning only confused him. In the midst of his turmoil, he suddenly realized he had never really asked for divine guidance in his efforts to establish a mission. His father had paved the way, help was available, and it had seemed the thing to do. He had seen no reason to question the validity of the mission.

Kenneth began serious talks with God: "Lord, what shall I do? Where did I go wrong?" He confessed his need for God's guidance. Then he waited to receive instructions from the Holy

Spirit, something he had not done before. Dad told us that it was the waiting that often caused people to give up their dependence on God. Every time we wanted to chart our own course, he would remind us that "asking is easy; waiting for the answer is difficult."

About this time, Ann had just about had her fill of "waiting on the Lord." She took her husband to task: "Kenneth, I think you've waited long enough. It seems to me God doesn't expect us to sit around defeated. It's time for you to put feet to your prayers and start knocking on doors. Haven't you preached to people that faith without works is dead?"

Her impatience stirred Kenneth to action. Now he approached God in desperation, "God, I've got to know why you haven't led me to do something or go somewhere. I can't move without your direction or I'll make the same mistake. You've promised to direct me and I need that direction now!" Kenneth felt a rise of his spirit, but whether from anger or from praying the prayer of faith he wasn't sure, until he started to get up and his line of vision fell on an old car across the street in Brother Abbott's backyard. His backbone stiffened. What right did Abbott have to own two cars when he didn't even own one and needed to get out and preach the Gospel! He got up and boldly strode out of the house and across the street to Brother Abbott's front door.

Faithful Brother Abbott never dreamed his old car could be commandeered to help preach the Gospel. It was all right with him if Kenneth needed it, but he warned: "It sure could stand some fixing up. The battery is gone, the tires are worn down, and it could use a new paint job—haven't used it in years."

Once Kenneth set his mind to a venture there was no difficulty he couldn't surmount, especially when he believed he had received direct guidance from the Lord. He told the church congregation of his need and the people caught the spirit of the venture. Donations came from dozens of people and soon the car was in tip-top shape, for an old car, that is.

Ann viewed this new approach for finding a pastorate with more than a few concerns, but if it brought results she'd be satisfied. Another young man in the church who also had a call to preach offered his services to repair and tune-up the car, providing he could go along to find himself a church, too. Kenneth always enjoyed the fellowship of fellow preachers; he welcomed his friend, considering his offer as an added blessing of the Lord.

Kenneth and Herman began traveling by faith on Saturday morning, heading their car south on Route 41. They arrived late in the afternoon at Attica, a good-sized town in western Indiana. It was a Saturday night town. Farmers were in town to shop and the streets were full of people strolling from store to store or just standing on the corner exchanging the latest gossip. Dad looked at the milling crowd and said to his friend: "Herman, we're going to have a street meeting here!"

"How? Who ever heard of two men holding a street meeting without music, or anyone to testify?" Herman frowned at the idea.

Kenneth answered, "Watch me." He dropped to the sidewalk on his knees and with a loud voice he started to pray with his arms stretched heavenward. When he finished he had his crowd. First, he preached; then his friend preached, and when they had preached themselves dry, they closed the meeting and stood watching the crowds slowly disperse wondering what to do next. Right then a bystander approached them with a solution.

"If you brethren have the time, our little mission is without a pastor, and we need someone to preach in tonight's service. If you have the time, it would be nice to have you preach for us."

The two street evangelists looked at each other—their eyes flashed the same thought: "Did they have the time?" They not only had time to preach, but they also took time to respond enthusiastically to an invitation to remain overnight for the

Sunday services. Kenneth was asked to preach again at the mission and Herman was directed to a nearby church needing a pastor. After the evening service, a quick conference took place between the deacons and the members and they decided to hold an election right then and there. Kenneth was unanimously chosen as pastor of the Attica Pentecostal Mission on the first ballot, and Herman came from his church rejoicing with the same news.

They took off for Hammond in a burst of praise to the Lord. Kenneth said they felt like Elijah taking off for heaven, except his chariot sped along on a puff of smoke rather than on a ball of fire. They sang, preached their finer points to each other, they shouted, and they laughed, and they wondered why preachers had a hard time finding churches. In the blaze of glory, his past failure faded; he could barely wait to tell his wife and father. How happy they'd be to hear of his instant success! Kenneth sighed with satisfaction and whispered a heartfelt prayer of thanks as they entered Hammond. Now at long last, he was Pastor Kenneth Wilkerson. It had to be God affirming his calling—of that he was confident.

CHAPTER 7

# LORD, WHAT NOW?

The first year as pastor of the small mission in Attica was a time of initial fulfillment for Kenneth. To be preaching and shepherding a people gave him great pleasure. He hoped they were people of faith. The parsonage, though small and without adequate kitchen facilities, had a spacious yard where the two children played. The congregation demonstrated their appreciation with offerings of vegetables from their gardens. The only drawback was the church's third floor location.

Kenneth's zeal for the ministry grew and his vision to do something worthwhile for the Kingdom of God preyed on his mind. Like his father, he could never be satisfied with the status quo and he was quick to share his dreams with the congregation. First, he prepared them with faith-building sermons and when he felt they had sufficient faith, he charged forward presenting a new program for the church. In this case, Attica needed a new sanctuary if they planned to increase the size of the congregation.

In each sermon, he thrust a challenge before them: "Folks, we sing 'Launch out into the deep—cut away the shoreline,' but what we really mean is: 'Lord, don't let it be too deep; it might cost me something.'" Powerful words, yet the task of convincing the congregation would not be easy.

The first hint of trouble brewing came from a member of the church who did not believe in tithing. Now, under Kenneth's

Spirit-anointed preaching, the man showed his true colors. In order to manipulate the congregation, the man began a "whispering campaign" to raise concern about the cost that would be imposed on the people. His goal was very evident—he must get rid of the pastor before the building program could begin.

Kenneth took such occurrences as personal affronts from Satan on the Church. Since he had no intention of being thwarted by someone who had been defeated by Christ, he boldly announced to the congregation: "Friends, I will not allow Satan to rear his ugly head in our midst."

With righteous anger, which he believed akin to the anger Christ demonstrated in the overturning of the temple tables, he preached right to the one being used by Satan. On this occasion, he chose an even finer technique for separating the "sheep" from the "goats."

"I want all those on the Lord's side to stand by the altar on my right, and all those on the devil's side to stand to the left."

The entire congregation, with the exception of the guilty member and his son, stood at the right. Even the man's own wife refused to stand against the pastor.

That night, in the home of the "goat," his wife had a dream. In tears, she woke her husband and told him she had seen him heading toward a precipice and he had fallen, screaming for help. Dreams and visions were very much a part of the Pentecostal faith in those days and the tragic scene struck fear into the heart of the husband.

Early in the morning, he rushed to the parsonage. When Kenneth opened the door, the man literally fell in the door begging forgiveness for his sin of gossip and causing dissension in the church. Kenneth led him in a prayer of repentance, and then laid hands on him asking the Lord to rebuke the work of Satan in the man's heart and set him free from satanic influence. The goat became a sheep and one of Dad's staunch supporters.

While some of the people fussed, fumed, argued and

complained, Kenneth went ahead with plans to build, even though the church's finances were stretched thin because of the Depression. Yet he determined to "launch out into deep water" even if few followed; he was that certain that God would bless their efforts.

God honored his perseverance and brought along a Christian contractor who offered his services without charge. But while the church building went up, the congregation slowly dwindled, and so did the finances, the gifts of food, and the general goodwill of the people. Soon there was little money, little food, and there were certainly no new members.

Years later, remembering those harrowing days of 1932 and 1933, Mother told us how God provided food for Juanita and David through a neighbor who not only invited them to play with her children, but also invited them to eat lunch and often supper, too. It was in their days of poverty that Mother learned to trust God for all their needs and to expect God's provisions to come in unusual ways.

Kenneth's first building program did not become the source of joy he had anticipated for the congregation or for himself. The attitude of the people toward making sacrifices to accomplish the vision of a new and larger church building, never matched that of their pastor and a group he called the "faithful sheep." Both Kenneth and Ann were physically and emotionally drained. Even the faithful were despondent. The only joyful event that year was the birth of Kenneth Gerald—who was nicknamed Jerry.

Hoping to revive the faith of the congregation, Kenneth called his friend, Gillam Lyon who had entered the evangelistic ministry, and asked him to preach a series of sermons.

Gillam remembers that first day of revival well: "Kenneth opened up the service and right off began denouncing the people, ending his short sermon by resigning from the church. Then he turned to me and said, 'Let's get out of here.' Hardly knowing what had happened, I strode out right behind him and my poor wife, completely bewildered, followed behind me while the audience sat dumbfounded."

Kenneth had reached his limitation of tolerance; he had no faith sermons left. Now he was no longer Pastor Wilkerson. Fortunately, before beginning the building program, he had rented his own house near the church, so at least they could not be forced from their home. But without an income, they could not eat, and they could not pay for a recently purchased used car—it would have to go back to the car dealer.

"Lord, what now?" It seemed to Kenneth that he was always praying this prayer. Because he had acted in a moment of anger, without consulting the Lord, it would be difficult to recognize the safest choice before him. He realized he had not yet understood what it meant to "walk in the Spirit."

Kenneth and Gillam talked over the situation. They both needed either a pastorate or churches in which to conduct revivals. There seemed to be only one choice—track them down. Ann and Cliffa, Gillam's wife, and the children were to stay behind. The Ohio District Council would soon be in session so plans were made to travel in that direction, seeking meetings in towns along the way to pay for the cost of the trip.

Off they started to points unknown. Thirty years later, when my husband and I were pioneering a church, I asked Gilliam to tell me the story of what happened after the "Attica incident." In response to my question, Gillam wrote the following story:

As we were cruising along at the lightning speed of thirty miles an hour, we suddenly saw a sign: PENTECOSTAL TABERNACLE. Right out in the country! We stopped of course. Inquiry revealed that a trustee lived in the vicinity. We looked him up and introduced ourselves. He invited us to stay and preach the next day, Sunday.

Now you can imagine our reaction when we learned we had stopped at a Free Pentecostal church. "Free" was a sure sign they took too much freedom in the Lord. Kenneth said: "We'll give them the straight Word. If they never hear it again, at least this time they'll get the truth." So we gave it to them.

First, I preached and in twenty minutes I was preached out; then Kenneth got up an opened both barrels. They didn't know what to do. They sat as though stupefied. He tried to make an altar call but they sat. He exhorted them again, and still they sat. Finally, he gave up and turned the meeting over to the leader. Well, the meeting sparked right up. They began to sing and then someone got up and began to dance; then more followed right out in the middle of the aisle. We sat while they shouted and danced. After a while they quieted down and the leader reached for his hat and coat. Then, as if it were an afterthought, he announced they would take up an offering for the visiting ministers to help them on their way. Kenneth and I were surprised but very much delighted. We thought that here was the answer to getting to the District Council, but when we counted the offering, we decided to abandon our venture and hurry back to Attica.

Again it was, "Lord, what now?" Kenneth was discovering hasty actions often are followed by desperate choices. They discussed their situation. They certainly would not go back to Hammond admitting another defeat. Gillam was Maxine's brother and was as determined as Kenneth to prove himself worthy of J.A.'s pastoral training. He had a car, so they packed all the furniture in one room, loaded the car with clothes and kids and headed toward Canonsburg, Pennsylvania, to the home of Ann's parents.

Grandmother Marton was a kind, generous person. With open arms she welcomed her daughter's family and their friends, although Grandfather Marton couldn't figure out why two ordained ministers could be without churches. Ann's sister, Helen, who had been converted under J.A.'s ministry, felt their sudden appearance a direct leading from the Lord. Her newfound zeal for serving the Lord gave her a burden for her own hometown and she had prayed for a Pentecostal church to be established.

Ann was pleased about pioneering a church in the town where her parents lived. The failures of the past dimmed as they moved toward a new challenge. While Gillam returned to Attica for their furniture, Kenneth arranged to rent a downtown building, and Ann scouted out an apartment for the family.

Kenneth would often warn people about the ways of Satan. "Just when things begin to go well, keep a lookout for Satan. He's not far behind, ready to put a wrench in the works." The relief of being settled in a place of their own turned to a torment. Unknowingly, they had become infected with scabies and the children were scratching and crying with the misery of the terrible itch. Their parents had the double misery of seeing their children suffer while they themselves were in pain. Helen purchased a medicine from the doctor who instructed them to mix it with lard; for three days and nights they lived in grease. Then the apartment, their clothes and the bedding had to be washed with lye soap. It was an ordeal not soon forgotten.

As was the custom of Kenneth, he approached God about their predicament, but before he could utter a word, Satan taunted: "Look at the mess you're in, God's punishing you for your failures. He doesn't care about you and your family. Why don't you curse God?" Kenneth had heard enough from Satan. He rebuked the adversary in the name of Jesus and claimed victory for his household. His bout with Satan ended the itch. Victory over discouragement and scabies had come by prayer and proper medication. Now they were ready to forge ahead in the Lord's work.

Gillam returned loaded down with their furniture shortly after the siege of illness. They were happy to see their friends, but there wasn't enough food in the house to prepare a full meal, with the exception of what had been sent from a relative in a gift package that very day. Overjoyed to be receiving a box, Ann had torn off the brown wrappings to discover a few odds and ends of clothing for the children and wrapped in a much needed raincoat, several apples. Yet, how they wished every stitch of clothing had been a box or can of food! What could two hungry families do with a few apples?

Ann came to the rescue. "I do have a little flour and just a speck of lard left. Maybe I could make a pie."

"A pie!" they shouted. They thought Ann had taken leave of her senses. With the bit of flour, lard, and the apples she produced a pie, proudly popped it into a tin breadbox to bake it over the stove's open flame, and then patiently watched over the pie until it had browned. She didn't know how it happened. She thought she had a firm grip on the pie, but there lay her prize, face down on the floor, smashed to a gooey mess.

Everyone stared in disbelief. Cliffa, the practical one reasoned, "Ann, the floor's clean." (It had been scrubbed that morning.) "Let's scoop it up and eat it." They did just that, and many years later they all remembered it as the best pie they had ever tasted!

With the help of Helen's money and Gillam's carpenter skills, they readied the hall for services. Gillam built a platform and pulpit. For fifteen dollars they purchased a piano, and even the mayor offered help by securing used theater seats for the hall. In a matter of a few days they were in "business."

But after months of effort and sacrifices, they felt the Canonsburg mission to be another exercise in futility. If it hadn't been for Helen and the Martons, they surely would have starved. Even so, there were days when stomachs groaned for lack of being filled.

In vain, Kenneth searched for a job. Did he dare approach God again for help? He did. He believed God would provide if he asked and believed for the answer.

A church in Findlay, Ohio, wrote to ask if he could hold a revival series for them. Since the Canonsburg mission had been at a standstill for several months, Kenneth took this invitation as a sign that God wanted him to move on. He traveled alone by bus, wondering if God was calling him to be an evangelist—he hoped not. He wanted to keep the family together. He prayed to find a pastorate so Ann and the children could join him.

In the warmth and safety of her parents' home where she knew the children would be well fed, Ann wrestled with disturbing thoughts. She had doubts of wanting to be in church ministry. She felt totally inadequate to meet the demands of a Pentecostal pastor's wife. Every pastor's wife she had met worked with her husband in the church, plus she was expected to raise children, keep a clean house, and entertain visiting evangelists and missionaries. She had dreamed of a career and of being independent—she had little interest in being a homemaker.

I don't think Ann talked about her problems with her mother. She had never communicated her troubling thoughts or emotional needs with her parents. They were Czechoslovakian immigrants and she viewed their way of living as old world ways; she wanted to live and think the American way. Becoming a Christian changed her attitude toward God and her family, but it did not change her long-standing habit of keeping her thoughts and problems to herself.

She had, however, developed the good habit of prayer and reading the Bible. I am sure that she found the comfort and guidance she needed through these means. Seldom did she share her inner struggles of those unsettling days. We do know, in spite of all the stress in her many roles, Mother remained faithful to Dad in his ministry. When she came to her "wit's end," she found a way to escape the stress—ironically it was taking periodic trips to her parent's home and finding peace and rest in their old world atmosphere.

## CHAPTER 8

# THE DEPRESSION YEARS

In the years of the Great Depression of the 1930s, churches that could support a family were not as available as Kenneth had hoped. The economic disaster within our nation affected every aspect of American life—including the Church. The Depression had made its mark on all denominations—and more so in the one Kenneth had chosen.

The Pentecostal denominations began establishing congregations in the early 1900s. They struggled against prejudice and ridicule for their belief in the baptism of the Holy Spirit as a second work of grace. Consequently, many of the Assemblies of God congregations were small and without adequate finances to enlarge their sanctuaries or support pastors with salaries equal to the average wage earner. During the Depression, they faced a greater financial crisis than the established churches since the majority of the congregations were made up of children and women who had no income.

When Kenneth set out from Canonsburg to hold revivals in Ohio in 1933, he faced an atmosphere of despair and hopelessness on the streets and within the churches. Because of his own difficulties, he could sympathize with people who were struggling to exist. Of those years, he later told congregations he had learned to preach to himself before he dared admonish people to have faith in God.

One of the churches where he held a revival needed a pastor. His one-week evangelistic revival did not bring the results he had hoped for; yet the people asked him to be their pastor. Against all good judgment on his part, he accepted the pastorate for the sake of the family. There was a reason he had hesitated—this particular congregation possessed what Kenneth called a "whooping and hollering" version of the Pentecostal experience of worshipping in the Spirit. Nevertheless, he moved the family into a second floor apartment and immediately searched for a job to support them.

While Ann braved the apartment roaches and rats, Kenneth braved a three-mile trek to earn a dollar's worth of produce for a daily wage. One day, the heavens shook with thunder and rain poured down on a very dejected preacher as he hoed the weeds. Suddenly a flash of lightening broke across the sky, knocking him to the ground. He lay on the ground, his heart pounding, wondering if he was alive. The jolt struck the deadness in his spirit, waking him to the realization that he was a child of God with a call to preach the Gospel, and instead he was fighting the elements and rodents, and fighting to stay alive. He stood up with a resolve to find a congregation who lived by the Scriptures and had a mind to build the Kingdom of God.

It was soon after his frightening experience that he wrote to his father to ask if he knew of churches needing a pastor. His father was a new pastor in Mansfield and not able to be helpful, but he did offer to negotiate for a Ford coupe so that his son could search for a stable congregation.

In the winter of 1934, they were facing one of their worst struggles. Christmas was nearing and the very thought of spending holidays in a cold apartment with little money to buy food or gifts for the children was more than the most saintly could endure. Thoughts of having the comfort of the family during the holidays ruled out their pride. For the children's sake, they took off for Mansfield hoping for a warm reception from J.A.'s family.

There was no royal welcome for one who had been gone three years and still had not found his place in the ministry. Kenneth's arrival with his family at this most inopportune season, bearing only tales of woe, didn't improve a father-son relationship. J.A., busy with raising a new family, found the sudden appearance of his son, for whom he thought he had done all he could do to launch him into ministry, to be a source of aggravation. And Kenneth was in no mood to withstand his father's grievances with him.

When he glanced at the gifts under the Christmas tree and did not see any for his children, it wakened past memories of his father thrusting him out on his own. He turned to Ann and said, "Get the children in the car." She obediently hustled Juanita, Dave and Jerry into the car without questioning. The visit hadn't lasted more that an hour. As they turned on to the highway, Ann dared to ask her seething husband: "Where are we going, Kenneth?"

"To your mother's," were his only words.

They drove to Pennsylvania in silence. Kenneth was too angry to talk. The pain of his whole life swept before him. His anger had been building up for a long time, and now it finally seemed to close the door on any kind of close relationship with his father. He made up his mind that he would never darken the door of his father's house again.

They arrived in Canonsburg tired, discouraged and very hungry. Grandma Marton had no idea they had left their church; she was just happy her daughter had come home for Christmas with her family. Grandma always prepared for the holiday season weeks in advance. There were all sorts of good things to eat and Grandma, with her "seventh sense," thought her daughter might show up and had a small gift for each of the children.

Happy to be home, Ann easily put the recent trials from her mind, but Kenneth could only sit and brood—he knew his anger had not been justified. J.A. had five children, and even though he had a growing church, he had financial struggles of his own during the Depression. He had given a great amount of his time and money into launching his son into the ministry and had responded to earlier calls for help. But Kenneth thought only of his feelings of rejection; he felt rejected by his earthly father, and now he harbored thoughts of the Lord abandoning his doubting servant. Mistake seemed to follow mistake.

The Martons wondered why their usually congenial son-in-law had become moody and unsociable. Kenneth could not bring himself to join in the merriment. Too much was at stake. Affairs between Kenneth Wilkerson and his God had to be settled once and for all, so off to the bedroom he went to "pray through." He had struggled too long with his problems, almost forgetting that God had a standing offer for His children to cast their cares upon Him and leave them there. He needed the Holy Spirit to set him straight about his relationship with his God and his father.

I can only imagine what he told the Lord. I'm sure he admitted the error of his haste and the sin of his anger, confessing that he had brought on their present tribulations by his own impatience. Now he sought God's forgiveness, asking for a renewing of his weary spirit. It may have been then that he forgave his father, for Kenneth never showed that he held a grudge, although he determined he would never again look to his father for any kind of assistance. He knew that it was time to trust his heavenly Father.

I recall Dad telling me, "Remember this, Ruth: God always loves you. He'll never reject a plea for help from one of His children." He discovered the promise of God's goodness and mercy during the most severe trials and tribulations.

Soon after the holidays, he continued his search for another church. Since he was not acquainted with the officials of the Pentecostal (Assemblies of God) churches in Pennsylvania, he did not know who to approach for assistance in locating a church.

One day, as he read the denomination's publication, *The Evangel,* a very unorthodox idea popped into his mind. The magazine listed churches announcing coming revival services and he had a strong urge to attend one of those churches. But which church? As long as he was going out on a limb with his extraordinary thought, he saw no reason for not going all the way.

As if not trusting his thoughts to be God's way of guiding, he brought Ann into the plan and asked her to pick the church. She closed her eyes, breathed a quick prayer for God to guide her finger, and then, without looking, she circled her hand above the page bringing her finger down to rest on a church in Pitcairn. A map revealed it to be a small town located near Pittsburgh, approximately forty miles north of Canonsburg. They both determined that was the exact church they must visit.

Leaving the children with their grandparents, they set out very early on a cold winter Sunday. They found the church in time to attend the morning worship service. The strangers did not go unnoticed in the small congregation. The discovery that Dad was a Pentecostal preacher immediately led to an invitation to be the guest speaker for the morning.

After the service, the people thanked Kenneth for the good sermon; some stayed to inquire about where they were from. Hearing he was in need of a church, one of the               members spoke up with a suggestion: "I heard there was a church in Cambria County needing a pastor. You might try there—the town is Barnesboro, but I can't say for sure that they still need a pastor."

Kenneth thanked the gentleman for this information and, after shaking hands with everyone, they went out the door to head home. Unknown to the pastor or the members, they had made the forty-mile trip on faith, with barely enough gas to get there and none for going back to Canonsburg. Kenneth had expected to be called on to preach—that was a common courtesy extended to a visiting minister in the Pentecostal churches, and an offering of some sort was customarily given to the speaker. Now they were walking away, their pockets empty, without one person having even suggested an offering. Just as they started to get into the car, the pastor came running down the church steps calling for them to wait. "Here, brother. The folks want you to have this." It was a five-dollar bill!

Kenneth and Ann were jubilant recounting the strange way they had been led to Pitcairn and given the name of a prospective church that they just might be able to call home. They were sure God had something special waiting for them in Barnesboro.

Anxiously they waited out the week. When Saturday arrived, snow was falling steadily, but they had set their minds making it to Barnesboro. They arrived late in the afternoon, made a few inquiries and at last found themselves at the home of one of the members of the congregation.

"Yes, we certainly have been praying for a pastor." The words of Sister Anderson were good news indeed. Kenneth wouldn't let himself become too hopeful even though their gracious hostess seemed overjoyed that he was available as a candidate.

Sunday morning, Kenneth stood behind the pulpit for his first service facing the small group of people who had braved the weather. By the end of the service, he knew he had come across a congregation with a mind to work with a pastor to build a strong Pentecostal church in their town.

He believed that the Holy Spirit had been guiding him to this point, even though he had faltered in his walk. He came to realize that his hasty actions had closed his mind to the Spirit's promptings. His prayer, asking God for forgiveness had again united his spirit in fellowship with the Lord. He thought of the patience of God in leading them to this church, and it set his spirit soaring with joy and gratitude.

After the benediction of the evening service, Kenneth asked the congregation to be seated. "Folks, I believe God has sent us to you. You are without a pastor and I am without a church. I would like to be your pastor." Amens could be heard simultaneously from the small group. They did not think it strange when he boldly requested: "Those who want me to pastor, please stand." To ask for a negative reply was unnecessary; the entire group immediately stood on its feet. Kenneth had at last found the church where he was truly needed.

They found a comfortable apartment in the home of Miss Thurston, who had inherited the house from her parents. Although she did not seem to mind three children, she soon became more than willing to rent them the entire house and move in next door with her sister. A few years later, she would have her house back, and three of us would return each week to her for a piano lesson.

I was born in the house on Philadelphia Avenue. My memories of living on that wide avenue are limited, and yet I do have one vivid memory of Granddad's family arriving for a visit and they didn't come alone or quietly. Three carloads of young people invaded our house with food and laughter. It seems Granddad had given a contest to raise money for the church building program and the winners were treated to a trip. I don't know if Granddad was rewarding his youth or wanting to show off how well his son had done for himself.

In the evening, they joined our congregation in a service. As always, it was Granddad's day. He completely overwhelmed us all with his joyous, charismatic personality. Dad happily stepped aside and let Granddad take control; he knew his father had a way of getting people to respond with enthusiasm. Granddad took out his banjo and walked back and forth on the platform, and sometimes down the aisle, encouraging people to make a "joyful noise to the Lord." The crowded sanctuary, the joyful singing, people kneeling at the altar to pray the sinner's prayer, plus the generous offering for Granddad's church, all prompted Dad to invite his father to conduct a fall revival.

Juanita (nicknamed Nan), David, Jerry, and I were

completely captivated by our relatives. It was our first contact
with Granddad and his family that we remembered, and we could
see they were something special.

"Boy, you should meet my granddad," Dave bragged the next
day in school. "He's better than any circus man. He can play and
sing and preach and do stuff with his leg." Dave was completely
enraptured by his unusual grandfather; he dreamed of being a
great preacher like his granddad, but he wasn't sure he could
swing his leg over the pulpit! Granddad added this demonstration
to his sermons on healing to shock the congregation to the reality
that miracles still happened. If it were a one-night visit to a
church he did it even if his sermon wasn't about healing.

Granddad stayed one day, just long enough to be satisfied
that his son had found a place in the ministry. Dad was the
shepherd he had always desired to become. At the end of the first
year, Dad wrote to his friend Gillam:

*I certainly do appreciate my past experiences. They have enabled
me to be an instrument in God's hands here. Our dear Lord has more
than made up for the lean years. I can hoe out the weeds now and
water the plants and have the pleasure of seeing them grow. Seeing the
Word take effect is a great blessing to me. God has been good to the
church…added twenty-five adults to our church roll…conducted a
good business meeting—one in which the Spirit of Christ was present,
and we were unanimously elected for another year. God alone knows
what the year will bring forth, but He will be with us come what
may.*

## CHAPTER 9

# COME WHAT MAY

One memory we all share is living in our very own three-story house on 18th Street in Barnesboro. Dad's salary increase made it possible for the household budget to allow his boyhood dream to come true. With money borrowed from the Marton's, Mother and Dad searched for a house with space for five children and a yard big enough to be a playground. They were so thrilled with the price and location of a large frame house on a quiet street that they didn't seem to notice several uninviting factors: the house needed paint and repairs, and the front yard had a well where miners, staggering home from an evening at a bar, stopped for a cold dousing down of their stupor before going home.

Dad would tell people: "When a congregation wants their pastor and his family to be blessed financially, it is sure evidence they have the Spirit of Christ." Dad's announcement that he had purchased his own home gave the church reason to show their generosity by giving gifts of money to buy furniture and make repairs. Eventually the budget would include a brand-new Chrysler in our driveway.

Like Good Samaritans, the church folks went beyond the call of duty and pitched in as if they owned the house. Women brought brooms and pails and cleaned the house from attic to basement. Brother Spike Wilson and young Danny Smith rolled up their sleeves and told Dad, "We've come to help, Pastor.

Where do we start?" David and Jerry pumped gallons of water from the well, while the men tried their luck at cementing a straight walk down the length of the backyard. The result was a masterpiece without a single crack and we children happily christened the job with our bicycles and skates. Mother captured this happy occasion in a snapshot for our family album.

When the major work was done on the outside of the house, the attic project began. This became a priority on the day my father opened the door of the middle bedroom and shouted down the steps, "It's a boy!"

I thought everyone showed baby Donald Wesley a bit too much attention. It was hard to relinquish my favored position after reigning for four years as the baby of the family. However, eventually jealousy faded when the three boys moved to the large attic and I moved into my own bedroom.

Our father made only necessary repairs and additions to the house; both Mother and he had learned the importance of being frugal in a parsonage—except when it came to a car and two new suits from Gimbel's in Pittsburgh every two years. Oh yes, and white shirts done by a professional laundry—a habit started in his Marine life.

In those days, Dad's salary was on a love-offering basis and woe to the pastor's income if he upset the cheerful givers! But in the heart of everyone—no matter how fervently one desires to be holy and stay in budget—lays seeds of extravagance. My father could not resist the purchase of a handsome combination radio and phonograph and albums of semi-classical records and southern gospel music, which we played during our evening meals.

Mainly, Dad wanted to keep up with the world news. On the weekdays we not only heard the call to prayer, we also heard the call to "Be quiet! Lowell Thomas is on." His deep voice sounded throughout the house so at an early age we learned current events. Keeping up with world news became a habit that all of us have adopted.

Mother's extravagance, piano lessons for each child, produced only one pianist in the family. Nan seemed to have the same love for music as Dad. My desire to be a world-known concert pianist faded into oblivion under the spell of books, and Jerry's cultural experience didn't last through his first music lesson. After Miss Thurston introduced him to his first piano book and instructed Jerry how to hold his hands over the keys, he simply said, "I don't want to," and walked out the door. To our anxious inquiries as to how he liked his first lesson, he nonchalantly replied, "Okay." It wasn't until David's turn that we found out the truth and I'm sure David wanted to walk out just as Jerry had done. He agonized through several lessons before getting the idea that saxophone lessons were more his style. Then the rest of us had to endure the weird sounds drifting out the attic windows. The greatest protest came from our dog who sat in the driveway howling through the practice.

Music, the only art we were encouraged to develop, was an integral part of church worship. Dad, through hymns and choruses, taught us to sing our praises to the Lord and proclaim the greatness of God. We sang about the death and resurrection of Christ, and of His eventual return for a Church "without spot or wrinkle." In devotional hymns, we unashamedly told Jesus that we loved Him and promised to surrender our lives to Him. We were challenged to go to nations to spread the Light, and to be like Christian soldiers marching off to war. Although we did not understand grace, this awesome truth was planted in our hearts when we sang of God's grace being greater than our sins. We had extraordinary spiritual encounters with God that were never experienced by many adults—and they were never forgotten.

Dad seldom permitted anyone to lead the congregation in singing. "That's when I take the spiritual temperature of the people," he would say. If they dragged the tempo, or sang without expression, he would stop and say: "All right, folks. Let's come to church. Ladies, forget about the dishes left in the sink, and, men, forget about your jobs. Let's worship God." He challenged the congregation to sing their best. When we ran out of hymns to express our feelings toward God, then we sang choruses. If a particular chorus touched hearts, we would sing the chorus again, lifting our hands to the Lord in adoration, or clapping our hands as an expression of our praise to God.

During the singing of the choruses, Dad invited the people to give a public testimony of God's recent blessings. Audience participation, which was woven throughout the services in various forms, brought much vitality to our services. No saint can refrain from sharing God's blessings: a thought may have burned within to encourage someone, a prayer may have been answered, and sometimes confessions were voiced publicly. During these "spiritual therapy" sessions, members would stand and testify and Dad would then choose a chorus to correspond with the testimony.

As children, we enjoyed this part of the service because Dad allowed us to request our favorite songs, too. But he never thought to explain to us that they had to be songs of the Church. During a revival service he became acutely aware of his oversight. The evangelist preached well, and the Spirit of God moved mightily upon the hearts of the people. The chorus and testimony time seemed charged with the presence of God. David was always receptive to the Holy Spirit and wanted to express to the Lord how much he loved Him. He shouted out one of his favorite school songs: "Let's sing 'Old MacDonald!'"

There was a moment of stunned silence. Seldom was my father speechless, but what could a preacher say to his son's sincere request. No one dared to laugh; only the pastor could direct his little parishioner into a better way of expressing his love to God. The congregation waited. Dad recovered quickly, a big smile told us he knew how to satisfy David. "Son, let's sing 'Jesus Loves Me,' a song that everyone knows." One big smile of relief seemed to envelop the people and they enthusiastically sang out for the children. Dave's grin and loud voice told the people that Jesus loved him, this he knew. "Old MacDonald" was left sitting in the barnyard!

Although a spiritual education, excelling in Bible, prayer, and music were of utmost importance to our family, our parents did believe in the value of a public school education. I found this out one cold winter day when the wind and snow blew fiercely and the furnace needed stoking. I stood shivering on the radiator declaring I was too sick to attend school. The pleasure of going back to bed lasted until the lunch hour when Mother informed me that I had to attend the afternoon classes and must give my first grade teacher the written excuse for the morning absence. I couldn't read what Mother had written, but I suspected it wasn't good when Miss Swanson displayed the excuse in a prominent place—she squeezed it in the upper left side of the door frame, and I had to look at it all afternoon with fear and trembling. As I put on my heavy winter clothing, she whispered in my ear: "Ruth, I know you will not let this happen again." And I never did!

However, a secular college education did not win approval with our parents, and neither Nan nor I were given support when we voiced our desire to attend a "worldly" college. For years, Dad steadfastly resisted our denomination's desire to change the three-year Bible institutions to accredited four-year colleges. He would not have a change of heart until 1957 when he reluctantly agreed to invite Robert Ashcroft, Director of Education for the Assemblies of God, to speak in the Scranton church where Dad was pastor at that time. He came for the sole purpose of convincing the congregation and the pastor of the need to support four-year colleges. At our dinner table after the Sunday morning service, Mr. Ashcroft spoke to Dad in his quiet and persuasive way, sharing with Dad his disappointment of being rejected as a chaplain during WW II along with other evangelical preachers because they lacked a college degree. Later, he had earned a degree and was able to convinced Dad of the importance of Pentecostal youth being in secular positions to bring spirituality into society. Years later, his son John would graduate from Yale, and go on to become our nation's Attorney General in 2001, and have tremendous influence in establishing laws to protect our country.

I readily admit that our Pentecostal background sometimes embarrassed me, and yet I must confess that there seldom was a dull day in our parsonage. In those early years, I do not recall being bored. During the summer months, we looked forward to Saturday evenings. This was our night out on the town with a small enthusiastic group from our church who held weekly street meetings in front of the bank on Main Street. We had our baths early and the boys slicked themselves up in case certain girls might see them. I could never understand why they bothered; they inevitably tried to escape the public shame of being seen with the Holy Rollers. I know, because along with the other little children, I was boosted up on the wide windowsills where I could see the older kids edging away from the group—my brothers leading the way.

For a long while, Tuesdays were the highlight of the week. Dad had been asked to preach once a week in the country church of Hellertown. We'd come home from school, hurry with our homework and then, one by one, we'd approach Dad with a request to please the heart of any preacher. "Dad, may I go with you when you go to preach tonight?" Dad was honestly too heavenly minded to see through our earthly desires. But we didn't fool Mother! She knew Dad loved ice cream cones as much as his children did, and that when we passed through the town of Patton, Dad would be sure to stop at the drugstore with an ice cream parlor. It became so automatic with Dad that we didn't even have to plant the idea in his head. In fact, we stopped there so often that he felt a burden to establish a Pentecostal church in

Patton and started street meetings in the town.

One of our most cherished memories of Barnesboro is of the family vacation. Where else would a minister like my father take his family but to a religious camp? To this day, the sound of a tolling bell stirs my memory of the camp bell calling us to eat in the dining hall. We children rushed in behind the adults who were singing, "Come and Dine." But to us, the invitation to come and dine and feast at Jesus' table meant "Let's eat! I'm hungry." Much later we grasped the real meaning to come and dine at the spiritual table where God had prepared an awesome feast.

At camp, I was captivated by the impressive parade of sights and sounds of Missionary Sunday. In my mind, I can still hear the drums and trumpets and voices thundering out "All Hail the Pow'r of Jesus' Name" and I see the missionaries slowly walking down the straw strewn aisle dressed in the colorful costumes of their adoptive nation, their national flags waving high as they assemble on the tabernacle platform. Each missionary gave moving testimonies of the power of God to "save" people in every land and of their willingness to sacrifice their lives for the Kingdom of God. They spoke of their call to the mission field and passionately urged young people to give their hearts wholly to Christ for His Kingdom. There were pleas not easily pushed aside.

David remembers camp for two reasons: it was the place of his calling into the ministry and it was also where he became self-conscious of his appearance. As he approached his teens he lost all the candy-bakery-store weight and now, according to his estimation, he looked more like a beanpole. He viewed his skinny physique with disgust, especially when he looked at Jerry with his dimples and curly blond hair. "The girls will never make eyes at me," he worried to himself. He began sporting his green corduroy jacket from morning to night to cover up his skinny arms. After a while, the jacket became a source of humiliation.

It wasn't easy to hit a ball encumbered with a jacket. No team captain wanted a teammate who couldn't roll up his sleeves and give the ball a good whack.

The jacket remained his cover-up until the graduation exercises on the last night of camp. The preacher's sermon caught David's attention: "I don't care what you look like—your outward appearance doesn't matter to God. It is what is inside that matters. God is looking for young men and women who will love Him with all their heart and mind and faithfully serve His Kingdom on earth."

David sat on the edge of his seat waiting to hear more: "God is calling some young person tonight. He wants to use you to reach thousands of souls for Christ's sake. All he asks of you is that you come and present your body as a living sacrifice for Him. You are never too young to make this consecration to God. Come, give yourself to God." Never before had the words of a sermon struck him as those did. He loved God and he knew God loved him; but to think that God could use him, that God actually wanted him—skinny and all—was an awesome revelation to David.

He could barely wait until the altar service. At the invitation to go forward, he jumped up, ran down the aisle and flung himself down on the straw. With arms raised up toward the heavens, he cried out: "Jesus use me. Put your hand on my life." A nearby minister placed his hand on David's head and prayed: "Lord, use this young boy for your service. Let him never lose this zeal and desire to serve you that he feels so strongly this night."

David got up, his face beaming. He had received "the call," the very same call that his father and granddad had received. No one knew that evening, not even David, how God would use him; but from that moment on, he was ready and willing to answer yes to whatever God asked him to do.

Dad was pleased to see David's desire for the ministry. He presented him with the book, Foxe's Book of Martyrs, with the solemn advice: "David, God always makes a way for a praying man. You may never be able to get a college degree, you may never get rich, but God always has and always will make a way for a praying man."

Nan, Jerry, and I cannot testify of receiving a call into ministry during our years in Barnesboro, but we do know that we each heard the same Gospel. We were taught the importance of prayer, and we were shown, by the example of our parents and church members, that to love God and believe Him was the highest measure of a person, and to serve God was the highest honor. We each chose our response to God according to our faith. We had an elementary understanding of God and a childlike faith, but the foundational stones given to us at that early age were strong for us to continue to build upon—if we chose to.

Amazingly, despite all its restrictions, our religious life brought us much happiness and security. Our pleasures were found in the warm and sincere fellowship we had with God, and with other believers. As children, we felt secure in the faith of our parents, we were happy just knowing we were loved by God and by our family. As long as we unquestioningly lived the faith taught to us, we lived in the security of believing that our lives pleased God.

It was when we were teenagers that our feelings of guilt began. We rebelled against the strict holiness teachings without sorting out which were traditions of our church and which were biblical commands. Like most teenagers, the five of us struggled with the faith of our parents, and each of us had to search out for ourselves the Truth, the Life, and the Way. Yet God pursued each of us, and as we studied the Scriptures, we came to realize the value of the wholesome home life that our parents and our church provided.

## CHAPTER 10

# PRAYERS OF A RIGHTEOUS MAN

My father revered the Bible as the only guide for living, and he regarded prayer as the greatest power given to man. He believed God had inspired the Scriptures and that the Holy Spirit causes the written Word to be effective in man. He believed God constantly communicates His will and purposes, and that the Holy Spirit assists us in receiving God's thoughts and in expressing our thoughts to God. In his sermons and in his journals, Dad talked about knowing the will of God. He did not think he had to search for the will of God, but believed instead that he must live in obedience to the Word so that he would be tuned to God's Spirit who reveals the will of God.

Dad studied and prayed in a room in our house. He referred to the room as his study—never an office. He studied many hours, searching the Scriptures and seeking to discover ways to apply the Word in a modern age. We could hear him pacing the floor and practicing his sermons out loud. It was Dad's prayer life that made him a forceful and inspiring preacher. Dad believed that the miracle of being reborn, the physical healing of the body, the loving response of God to people's needs, and fellowship with God on a personal basis all happened through prayer.

In his journal, he comments about his prayer life: "I find the day goes much easier if one meets God in the morning." Because Mother couldn't drive, it became one of Dad's duties to take her to the grocery store; even though he took a book along to read while she shopped, he commented: "I am jealous of everything that keeps me from His presence." At one point, he hoped to resolve being Mother's chauffeur by giving her a driving lesson, but both were so nervous that the lesson ended in a ditch and the scare of it lasted for years.

The importance of biblical knowledge and communication with God was instilled in us from the day we were born. We were only a few days old when Dad took us into his arms and dedicated us to God at the altar of the church. While other children were going off to dreamland to the sound of lullabies, we slumbered to the sound of hymns and our father's sermons. As we grew older, we began to take part in the services. Certain truths in the hymns and in our father's sermons stayed with us— and still do until this day.

Prayer at the altar followed every worship service. They were concerts of audible prayers to God by the entire congregation, including the children. All five of us knelt at these altars. We learned to pray by watching and listening to our elders. We poured out our love to God with simple expressions of worship; we made sincere dedications of our lives to serve in His kingdom when we grew up. Sometimes we cried tears of repentance, especially when we knew we had committed a transgression.

Family prayer was the mortar for our family togetherness. When the time for prayer came, Mother dispatched the nearest child to round up the others. The entire neighborhood became accustomed to hearing Jerry bellowing out: "Come on home! It's time to pr-a-ay." Immediately we stopped playing and headed for the living room. Our parents never had to explain the importance of prayer. The very fact that it was done daily, without fail, made us respect the sacredness of family prayers. I don't recall one of us refusing to join the family in prayer. I think we all rather cherished these special times because it was one of the few times we prayed as a family.

Mother used a variety of ways to "hide" the Word within our hearts. She challenged us with stories from Bible storybooks that made the ancient people of the Bible come alive. Our heroes were Moses, Joshua, David and a host of other biblical men and women. We listened intently because Mother would be sure to ask questions on the lessons and each one of us prided ourself in being the smartest Bible scholar.

Then together we knelt, with the living room sofa and chairs as our altars, and Dad prayed. He called us each by name before God. Chills of awesomeness would still our hearts as he prayed:

*God, bless Juanita. Remind her of your Word that she has learned around these altars. Help her to learn to trust you. Lord, use David mightily for Your Kingdom. Help him to trust in the power of Your Spirit and not in his own strength. And Jerry, Lord, watch over him; may your Spirit be with him letting him know of your love for him. Bless Ruth, and use her for your service as you have used handmaids of old. And Don, our youngest, Lord, make him a preacher of the Gospel.*

Blissfully, we scrambled up from our knees to go off to school or play, but not for one minute did we doubt that God heard our father's prayer. When we were alone with our thoughts about life, we talked with God from our hearts, putting words to our desires, promising to serve in His Kingdom—often as a missionary in a foreign country. It seemed such an easy commitment to make when we were young.

Both Mother and Dad had their private prayer times each day as well. We took for granted the sounds of fervent prayer flowing from the lips of our parents, permeating the house with the presence of God. We walked quietly, as if on holy ground, when we heard them pray. If we tiptoed past their doors, we could hear our names mentioned. It never failed to fill me with reverence for God. At an early age, I became aware that God knew me by name. Hearing my parents pray increased my desire to pray and to be good. To this day I am strengthened by the potency of their prayers; it is as if I can still hear my name being called before God.

Maybe the prayers of our parents kept us from earning the usual preacher's kid label of being rascals. But we did have several memorable spankings in our Hall of Shame; one of the most deserving was bestowed upon Dave.

It seemed Dave would never accept his responsibility for doing dishes. "That's a woman's job," he'd fuss every time it was the boys' turn. Mother felt that this was the least the boys could do to help in our busy household, so his fuming went unnoticed until he took matters into his own hands. "I'll show them," he told Jerry one morning. "I'm leaving home and they'll be sorry they ever made me do a dish." Off he traveled. He roamed the streets until his feet ached. Then wearily he climbed Baldy Hill to look down at the house hoping to see the effect of his rebellion upon the household.

"He'll be back," Mother had confidently informed us; but supper went by and there was no sign of Dave. The three of us formed a posse and searched the neighborhood. Finally, Dad decided to ride around, hoping to find him before dark. Dave looked down and saw the beginnings of our anxiety and smugly rejoiced to himself: "I'll bet they'll appreciate me after this."

He stayed out long enough to give us all a good scare and then came marching triumphantly down the hill, ready to receive the Prodigal Son's welcome; but there was no supper, and no merry-making. We all ignored the one who had dared to punish us for his act of rebellion. Even though Mother knew he was tired and hungry, she offered not a morsel of food. Dave sat brooding on the front porch swing while we hung around sufficiently out of sight, waiting for the action to start. Finally, Dad walked out the front door and said, "All right, Son, up to the bedroom." As always, King Solomon's rule of discipline brought about a painful but peaceful settlement.

Invitations to the homes of church members were occasions of togetherness for our family, thanks to such wonderful people as the Smiths, the Greenaways, and the McGees. We were greeted royally and treated to foods never served on our table. After the supper hour, the grownups met in the living room to talk over spiritual matters and sometimes politics, while we played together with our friends. When Mother announced, "We're going to pray now," we knew it was time to leave. Dad never left a home, no matter how long or short the visit, unless he prayed for the physical and spiritual needs of the family and asked God's blessing upon the household. At a young age, we became aware that people had real needs and that if we prayed for people, God would help them. It was the beginning of learning to "bear one another's burdens."

Prayer during church board meetings was done primarily to seek God's direction in church matters, but David recalls one time in Barnesboro when Dad used prayer for protection. It is a known fact that even saints have disagreements, possibly because we are never as saintly as we think we are. When the disagreeable are the carnal-minded, the Word usually corrects their tendencies, but when the disagreeable are the self-righteous, they will not allow the Word to penetrate their wall of pride. As the Barnesboro church prospered and grew, new members were added and, even though Dad maintained a strict membership code, somehow those "goats" always managed to mingle with the sheep.

Even as children, we could recognize these folks as they proudly displayed gifts of the Spirit or gossiped about the preacher, or had their own interpretations of the Scriptures. We all remember the name of the lady who would interrupt Dad's sermons with her utterance in an unknown language because she was the source of trouble. Her gossip about the pastor and the church members knew no boundaries. Dad counseled her in a roundabout way by teaching about the misuse of gifts and the pattern Apostle Paul had laid out to the churches to avoid such pride. But it was to no avail.

In the midst of these troublesome days, Dad called for a special board meeting to deal with some of the gossip. One of those members, the husband of the woman, was heard to say: "I'll beat the tar out of the pastor. How dare he call my wife carnal and self-righteous and say her gifts are not of God!" Dave overheard Dad tell Mother, "They're out to get me this time, but they can't hurt me. I've got God to protect me."

Dave wanted to tell Dad, "You've got God and me. I'll be there to help you." But he knew Dad would only thank him for his concern and tell him God would take care of him. Dave just wasn't sure, and if Dad might have to go through peril like the Apostle Paul, he meant to see that Dad was rescued from such tribulations. From the basement he armed himself with a football helmet and a rusty sword left from the previous tenants; then, with lightning speed, he ran through the back alleys, beating Dad and the Board to the church.

By huddling in the coal bin where the cold-air return from the sanctuary would be just above him, Dave was able to hear every word being said. He heard the footsteps of Dad, then the slow heavy pace of six men behind him. They were gathering at the altar. He heard Dad's strong, deep voice: "Brethren, I think we need to begin this board meeting with prayer around the altar." The seven men knelt and Dad prayed. He peppered his prayer with all kinds of Scriptures about the dangers of touching God's anointed; he reiterated the tragedy of those who murmured and complained in the Israelite congregation. Though the board meeting ended with brotherly hugs and David was able to put away his weapons, the undercurrent of gossip remained because of the sister's insistence of her righteousness and repeated demonstrations of speaking in tongues in every service.

David did not know the gossiping started among a few people while Dad was in the hospital for an operation on his ulcerated stomach. Dad became anemic because of loss of blood and had experienced a dark low in his body and his spirit—he wondered if he would live through an operation. Much prayer went up to God on his behalf by the members who were truly saintly; but the gossipers began to criticize Dad for having the operation. They viewed his constant bouts with bleeding ulcers as a lack of faith—the operation proved this to be true in their estimation. One of the women refused to allow Dad to pray for her when she was sick. She spread the idea that he could not possibly have the faith to believe for her healing.

While they continued their "gossip campaign" against Dad, he started a prayer and preaching campaign, inviting an evangelist whom he believed would help to bring about a change in the discordant members. In his journal Dad recalled, "The first night of the revival was fairly good. I believe God is going to meet us if the people will respond. Brother Shearer is an old-timer—chops his own wood, lets chips fall where they may." By this, Dad meant that the evangelist would be like John the Baptist and tell the people the truth about their sins.

The next day he expressed his feelings about the wayward group: "I was moved with compassion today for the carnal babies of our flock. Sister B. shows some improvement, but a character such as hers cannot change overnight." But then the next day he reports that Sister B. tried to take over the service with a display of her "gift" of tongues and the evangelist told her to "hold it." Dad prayed: "Lord, give me wisdom to deal with her."

On Easter Sunday morning, he again recorded his hopes: "I trust the carnal folks will really get religion in this revival...but I'm afraid some people won't come clean." Some of them did, but not Sister B.

Dad also records an extraordinary confession of a man who

had stolen money from a credit company years before, and could not make peace with himself and God until he made provisions to return the money. Dad and the evangelist drove the man to Pittsburgh to make restitution. The company officers were so touched by the man's confession they decided to forgive the offenses. Dad reported that the man's daughter became a Christian upon hearing about the change in her father.

Men and women began to voluntarily stand before the congregation to confess their guilt of gossiping, or they came knocking at our door to make their peace with Dad. I sat on the stairwell steps listening; when it came time for prayer, I ran to my bedroom and prayed for the people, too. Yet, with all the prayer and confessions Dad wrote about a "depression that seems to settle over the services" and he determined to help the people learn to shake off their guilt and to praise God for His grace and mercy. Even though he had prayed and preached and people had made things right with God and with him, he wrote: "I am sure now God is through with me in Barnesboro. I long for a new battle, and to be used in a greater way for my Savior."

Dad had not yet fully recovered from the operation. He wrote in his journal: "It is not my lot to have a strong body, but I will give my Lord the best I have." Still he kept up his strenuous task of shepherding the flock, ignoring his loss of weight and strength and the gnawing pain in his stomach, praying that God would send him to another congregation. He hoped some other pastor could show the sister the error of her ways; he felt he had done all he could do.

When the answer to his request arrived, it came from such an unexpected source, and seemed so uninviting, that Dad refused to believe the call came from God. Actually, it was not a direct invitation from a church but a plea for help from the son of one of the Barnesboro parishioners, who told Dad of the little church he was attending and that they "sure needed faith-building sermons" like the ones he preached.

An invitation from a small church that had split off from a larger church over doctrinal issues did not seem like an answer to Dad's prayers for a flock of "sheep." Dad told Mother: "I don't think God expects me to take the family into such a situation." For the second time in my father's life, he did not pray about the call, he simply threw the letter in the wastebasket.

Several months later he lay dying as the result of internal bleeding caused by the operation on his stomach that had not healed. Steadfastly, Dad had refused to believe he was seriously ill; but he had suffered a great loss of blood and the doctor's prognosis was not good. A second operation was needed to stop the hemorrhaging.

The five of us lined the upstairs hallway waiting for the sound of the ambulance. Our hearts were frightened and broken as we heard Mother praying that God would spare Dad's life while Dad could be heard calling out strange things.

"Why does he keep talking about the beautiful flowers," I kept asking Nan.

"Because he's hallucinating," was her bewildering reply.

We watched with tears streaming down our cheeks as the funeral director, who was also the ambulance driver and Dad's friend, tenderly carried him down the stairs.

David sobbed as if his heart would break; he put his arms around Mother and told her, "Don't worry, Mom. If anything happens to Dad, I'll go to work and take care of you." Through her tears, Mother gratefully whispered, "Thank you, Son."

The prayers of the congregation Dad had so unstintingly served for ten years brought about a miraculous deliverance. The doctor's only comment was: "It had to be God." He had not had much hope for his patient's recovery.

Slowly, Dad regained his energy, and his resolve to leave Barnesboro became all the more intense when he learned that the gossip campaign had continued while he was hospitalized.

Dad came home from the hospital firmly believing that his

trial of sickness could have been avoided had he responded to that invitation from the small church. He based his beliefs on stories of God's dealings with the Israelites: each time they rebelled against God's instructions, they brought punishment upon themselves. Dad believed God had punished him for refusing to obey. In those days, neither Mother nor Dad had a deep understanding of the grace of God. Their distorted view of God became a source of an unfounded fear of God for all of us. And yet, Dad trusted in the goodness of God to work all things together for good.

No sooner had he made his promise to God to consider the small church, when again the persistent young man wrote, urging Dad to reconsider the invitation. This time Dad sat down at his desk to pen an immediate reply: "Yes," he wrote. "If your church Board wants me for a candidate, please set a date and I'll be there."

On May 2, 1945, an entry in Dad's journal gives us a look into the measure of his faith and the constant stress of a weak body: "The weather is still bad, which does not help my frail body. I am enjoying day-by-day fellowship with my Lord, but find the uncertainty as to where He will lead to be hard on me. May He help me to rest wholly upon Him! Visited with the McGees in evening—retired feeling better in my soul."

On Sunday, the 6th, he recorded the day of his resignation: "Read my resignation this morning. Everyone, except possibly the (two carnal families), were sad and cried very much. I exhorted at length on being faithful to the church (in Barnesboro) and recited the nature of my work here through the years. Preached on 'Running from God' in the evening—some of the guilty ones feel like running—getting away."

Dad was leaving ten years of fruitful ministry and ten years of learning experiences. He would tell us that God always prepares a person in advance for the work he or she is to do, whether it be in the church or in secular work. Dad believed he was up to the new challenge.

    We had spent ten years in a small community that provided us with an excellent public school education and despite the strict holiness rules, we were given exceptional spiritual training. We may not have been given social tools, but we each knew how to communicate with God and we understood He had very real plans and purposes for our lives—something, I discovered, that school mates seemed totally ignorant of. We may have been different, but in an awesome kind of way!

# THE CHURCH IN TURTLE CREEK

We were all excited about moving. We suddenly were noticed in our school because of the great occasion. Not many kids in Barnesboro moved out of the small community. It was sort of a phenomenon. We became instant celebrities among our peers.

We were moving to Turtle Creek, a small suburb of Pittsburgh. The odd name dampened our anticipation of moving. Who could enjoy living in a town named after a turtle! We quickly agreed to call our new home T.C. Had we known the shocking facts Dad purposely left out of his description of the town and church, we certainly would have vetoed the move by a unanimous vote. Only the description of our new abode sounded worse than the name. After a grand tour of T. C., we all expressed the same feeling: "No wonder Dad threw the first invitation in the wastebasket." We soon wished he had done the same with the second letter.

Yet, just as Apostle Paul felt compelled to answer the Macedonian call, so Dad believed God called him to T. C. He laid claim to the promise: "I can do all things through Christ, who strengthens me," and believed, that with God's help, he could tackle the problems of this needy church and be given the physical strength for a building program.

Turtle Creek was "all things." It was a dirty town nestled among Westinghouse factories. It was a church in a former auto shop located in the flood area of the town and situated almost underneath a railroad trestle. It was an apartment parsonage above the "sanctuary" with no place for children to play. It was a group of forty people who had split off an independent church. It was a decrease in salary for Dad, which meant meager times for us all.

Dad had made one stipulation before accepting the pastorate. He would not raise his family in the apartment that was to serve as a parsonage; however, the limited income of the church meant selling the Barnesboro house and investing in another. To his dismay, he discovered houses in the area cost three to four times as much as the house he owned in Barnesboro. The sale of our house would only provide the down payment; once again Mother's parents came to the rescue with an interest-free loan. Nevertheless, Dad knew that the hardships of the T. C. ministry would be great enough without subjecting his family to poor living conditions. So the search for another home began.

We were pleased with the house our parents had chosen, but we were positive we would never like T. C. It was a sacrifice we were making for our father, so for a while, the five of us hung together, wary of the neighborhood kids curious about the new family on the block. Dad and Mother didn't seem to be hampered by fear or pride; they wholeheartedly took to city people and city life. But we five "hillbillies" disdainfully held ourselves apart from city slickers who boldly presented themselves to us for our friendship. The truth of our pride was, we were so uninformed about city life that we were downright ashamed of our small town roots, and we were not accustomed to the worldliness that seemed to thrive all around us.

When I was young, the words of Christ: "My prayer is not that you take them out of the world but that you protect them from the evil one," were interpreted by most Pentecostals to mean we were to live among the sinners yet keep ourselves almost totally out of the affairs and pleasures of the world. Because no set rules were listed in our doctrines except the forbiddance of smoking, drinking and gambling, they varied from church to church, from family to family, and with time.

During our teen years, our parents expected us to follow the rules already instilled in us. We were permitted the friendship of classmates, but not the privilege of attending school activities. Neighborhood sports made the list, but not professional or high school games. Movies and amusement parks were definitely on the "no" list. Modern modest clothes passed inspection, but not makeup or jewelry. Our social activities were limited to church affairs and neighborhood sports and games.

I was shocked by the realization that we had lived a very sheltered life in Barnesboro. I had never imagined a world such as this: there were school activities galore and an abundance of worldly friends who didn't think it strange to associate with Pentecostal preachers' kids. The youth of our church took part in worldly activities and their paths of pleasure beckoned us; we soon were at odds, not with our church, but with our parents.

While sports were still on the condemned list, they became the worldly downfall of Dave and Jerry. They obediently viewed the football games from a hill above the stadium and this sufficed while they were novices about the things of the world. A year later, when we were all sophisticated city people, the boys boldly confronted Dad for some answers: "Why can't we go to the games? Is playing ball in a stadium a sin?" It was one of the few times the boys questioned the rules, and they stood waiting for Dad's answer. "I guess there really isn't any sin involved," he said. "You may go on one condition; these ball games must never keep you from attending church." The boys were elated. T. C. wasn't so bad after all. In fact, T. C. was the greatest! And in that moment, Dad was, too!

Don vividly recalls an incident that taught him not to

challenge certain rules. He had made arrangements to meet a girl friend in the city and treat her to the delights of Kennywood Park, Pittsburgh's largest amusement park. Don had made the forty-five minute trip by streetcar with Dave and Jerry, but this was his first venture into the city alone. Because of his destination, he dare not ask permission to make the trip; he simply went, never thinking that his deed might be found out. He arrived at the meeting point a half-hour early. A tent across the street drew his attention, especially when he discovered a sign announcing nightly healing services. He walked across the street and sat in the tent to wait out the time in a more secure location than the busy street corner. The day had been windy; suddenly the wind blew with hurricane force. With a loud swish, the large tent lifted from its stakes and began descending like a parachute, down upon the seats.

Thankfully, Don had chosen a seat in the back row and easily made an escape. He ran back to the street corner trembling and almost in tears, realizing had he been sitting in the middle of the huge tent—he could have been killed. Don met the girl and they had their thrills on the rides, but Don's mind was not at peace. Conviction settled down upon his heart just as the tent had slowly settled on the ground. He had to make a confession to ease his mind. Just telling his girl wasn't enough. A convenient confessional box stood nearby; it was marked TELEPHONE. He paid the dime and made his confession to his father: "Dad, this is Don."

"Where are you?" a phone call from his youngest son was unusual.

"In Pittsburgh!" Don replied in a hushed voice.

"What are you doing there? How did you get there?" Now alarm bells went off in Dad's mind. Don had traveled too far from home.

Out came the story of a disobedient son. The lecture Don received wasn't half as bad as the lesson he had learned. That episode was as close to rebellion as he ever got. He planned to be a minister and he wanted to be as good as his father.

Mother and Dad were challenged to make changes in their holiness standard by the demand of our needs and by a congregation who had not been indoctrinated with Granddad's ideas of holiness. A few pleasures that the Barnesboro membership frowned upon were gradually eliminated from the condemned list. After a while, we all could attend the school sports events and the boys were given freedom to sightsee Pittsburgh with friends. They probably bought more peanuts at the zoo than any other preachers' kids in Allegheny County.

Eventually, when they became wage earners, Dad agreed that the boys had proved that they were responsible and allowed them to attend professional baseball games at Pittsburgh's Forbes Field. To keep us occupied at home, Dad dug into his limited income to provide us with a ping-pong table, and he nailed up a basketball hoop on the garage. For the boys, these activities were enough, for they were the very things they liked to do. Working after school and on Saturdays kept them out of a great deal of mischief, and it also gave them the satisfaction of being financially independent.

But, alas, as a girl, I had to find satisfaction in less adventurous activities. It was no fun watching my brothers and my friends go off for a good time with dates, so I sought what seemed a very natural escape—reading. I think I read most of the books in the school libraries. The books I especially enjoyed were my sister Nan's Grace Livingston Hill's Christian romance novels. Books took me into a world of adventure and set my mind dreaming of how I would live after leaving home. Romantic dreams were patterned after the stories in the novels. I had my heart set on a "knight in shining armor" who loved God and had lots of money—a modern day Boaz.

Marriage happened to be one of my father's favorite subjects. He took delight in playing the role of matchmaker and history records several happily married couples that said, "I do," thanks to his art of matchmaking. Dad had definite ideas—some based on Scripture, plus a few prejudiced from his days as a Marine. Automatically, when I became interested in a fellow, Dad's philosophy would pop into my mind: "Look at his shoes. A man of breeding keeps them polished. Be not unequally yoked together. Is he a gentleman? How does he treat his mother? That is the way he will treat you. Does he enjoy the things of life that you do? Does he serve God?" That was quite a list. I wondered if such a man existed.

Nan entered her junior year of high school when we moved to T.C. In those two years before her graduation, our family had a difficult time of adjustment. The holiness rules were beginning to be challenged, especially by Nan. Mother and Dad were not ready to loosen the rules so Nan began to openly rebel. We never sat down together as a family to express our thoughts and feelings about the rules—this simply was not done. Looking back, I think our parents believed they were parenting according to God's rules, and that left absolutely no room for discussion, but it did foster rebellion. Nan would no longer accept the lectures; she determined to do as she pleased. Unfortunately, one day she broke a cardinal rule and did not show up for church, a rule none of us dared break.

By now, Dad had reached his limit of knowing how to cope with a rebellious child and without giving it enough thought, he reverted to his old way of discipline. He spanked Nan when she was sixteen and from that day on she set her spirit against Dad and the Pentecostal church. Dad had broken one of the rules of the Scripture to not exasperate children to the point of resentment. He would forever regret his method of correction. It only served to give Nan more reason to rebel.

Financial struggles in those two years added to our family troubles. The family had needs that Dad's salary could not meet, and the mileage on his car warned him of its impending demise.

There were house payments to meet and house repairs to be made. Things were desperate. We heard prayers coming out from his study and we knew they were pleas to God for help.

None of us would have dreamed God would send an evangelist who would help meet some of the financial needs— especially not a woman evangelist. Mother had always been opposed to women preachers, and in particular, women who taught the "deeper life" experience. It sounded like more holiness restrictions to Mother. Somehow this woman got past Mother and for good reason.

Sister Harkins lived near T.C. and owned a corner grocery store with her husband. Hearing of the financial needs, she offered Dave a job in their store. Jerry later received the same offer. It meant that the boys had to rush home from school, quickly eat, and then run down the hill to take a streetcar to work. Their schedule did not leave much time for pleasures, but the jingle of money in their pocket compensated for the loss of a normal teenage life. It also taught the boys the responsible "work ethic" our father preached about, and it prepared Jerry for an eventual career in the grocery business.

Dad had new experiences, too: he was appointed as a Board member of Eastern Bible Institute where Don and I would attend. His greatest honor came when he was elected Presbyter of the Northwest Section and found great enjoyment as a mentor to young ministers and assisting in church plantings. He also found himself defending a healing evangelist named Kathryn Kuhlman, who generated a great deal of publicity with her dramatic preaching style and unusual healing services held in Carnegie Hall in Pittsburgh.

After attending one of her services, Dad was among the few Pentecostal ministers who returned with a good report. In spite of her known divorce and the fact that she "dressed up for Jesus" with lipstick and earrings, Dad believed that the Holy Spirit worked through her and people were healed. Dad suggested to fellow ministers to adopt a "wait and see" attitude instead of condemning her before their congregations.

Dad proved to be right in his assessment of Miss Kuhlman's gifts. Years later, David received an invitation to speak in her healing campaigns about his work in Teen Challenge and she donated generous financial support to his ministry.

Except for Nan, we were appreciating suburban living and the positive changes in our life style. We no longer looked back to the "good old days" of a quieter time. We were learning to cope with the challenges of growing up in a city environment, on a limited income, watching our parents struggling with the many problems of establishing a congregation and one in need of a new place of worship. Like the town's name suggested, Dad's work in Turtle Creek would move slowly and require a great amount of energy and courage to see his goal of a new church building and a growing congregation working together in unity.

## CHAPTER 12

# THE FAITHFUL SERVANT

In my home library, I have several black notebooks that I cherish. They contain sermons that Dad wrote in longhand in the days before he owned a typewriter. There doesn't seem to be a subject that he missed. His sermons give the reasons for many of his decisions. I often wonder why he believed God required him to move to T. C. Those eleven years were a continual life of sacrifice for our family. Dad had to leave the fat years for the lean years. It also meant that he could not put away any savings for his retirement, much less think of sending any one of us to college.

Dad's sermons give the key to his willingness to make sacrifices for the sake of the Gospel. In almost every sermon he speaks of the honor of serving Christ and of the eternal rewards for the faithful servant. In those times, Pentecostal preachers spoke more about future rewards than present day ones. He explained his focus using Apostle Paul's example of running the Christian race to win, always pressing toward the mark for the prize of his high calling. The hope of eternal rewards sustained Dad; he saw no reason to complain. He planned to live forever.

When it came to the work of the Lord, Dad had a strong faith and a great amount of spiritual endurance. His patience with church members, Board members, fellow ministers, and even with our parsonage economy were greater than his patience with such trivial things as misplaced household tools or with Mother when she cooked the same breakfast three days in a row. His positive outlook upon the ministry helped him survive the pressures of the T. C. church. He refused to allow his point of reference be on the small congregation or a small salary. Dad had his eyes on a hill beyond the church far above the train trestle. There on the corner of the block where members of the town board and town merchants lived, stood an empty piece of land no one wanted. The lot itself rose in a mound of earth and no builder wanted to conquer the tons of dirt or the solid rock hidden beneath.

"Folks," Dad announced after preaching for a year on launching out in faith, "when you leave the church today, look up to the hill above and believe that God is going to put us there someday. That corner is seen from every hill in our city. We'll be a shining light to the glory of God."

It took five years of preaching sermons on courage and faith—to himself as well as to the congregation—and five years of sacrificial offerings before the building of a new church could begin. The town laughed when Dad hired a bulldozing company to knock down the hill. "You'll never dig a foundation out of that stone," they scoffed. The huge shovels easily dug the dimensions for the basement and had to stop. There was no need to go any further—they had reached solid rock. On that rock they built the church.

The church was not as grand as those I passed on the way to school, but we gained notice and prestige by being situated in an upper, middle-class neighborhood. But still we were regarded differently than the traditional denominations. Neighbors expected to hear shouting and loud singing, and maybe if they dared peek in, they might see people dancing in the aisles or rolling on the floor! None of that happened in the T.C. church. Dad liked joyful singing and he encouraged people to audibly praise the Lord, but he aimed for a genuine work of the Spirit in the hearts of people. When anyone went beyond those boundaries, Dad reminded them that they were in control of their choice of worship.

But he couldn't control Granddad the day he stepped into the pulpit of our new sanctuary. He arrived on a chilly, rainy day and had worn rubber boots over his dress shoes. Dad had invited him to preach that evening; he knew something was up when his father carried his boots to the pulpit.

Sure enough, when Granddad stepped up to preach he took his muddy boots and placed them on the altar. He was about to give us an object lesson on becoming too prideful of our new church and of moving to a more affluent neighborhood. He informed Dad and the congregation that if we were going to make good use of our building, it might get a bit dirty. And why not let the neighbors know we were alive and ready for business?!

Without consulting Dad, he instructed the deacons to open the windows and proceeded to lead the congregation in an old-fashioned, Pentecostal "Jericho March" around the perimeter of the pews while we sang chorus after chorus, clapping our way to victory over pride. The neighbors knew we were alive that night—and so did we! As usual, Granddad left us with a dramatized sermon we did not forget.

During those eleven lean years, we all had to find our own way to ease the financial burden put upon us by our father's vision for the congregation. We also bore the effects of the stress put upon our parents: there would be no camp vacations, no family outings at country farmhouses, and no escape from helping to shoulder the financial needs of the family. The saddest loss for me, because David, Jerry, and Nan were working, we no longer met for family prayer and we seldom sat around the dining room table for a meal together. In very real ways, what little family bonding we had in Barnesboro, ceased to exist in T.C.

Another change (but less significant) sat in our driveway. Dad could no longer afford a Chrysler. Instead, according to the neighborhood kids, he now drove an upside-down bathtub: we were humiliated with having to ride in a Nash. We let Dad know that we did not approve of his economizing on a car. David solved his disappointment by investing twenty-five dollars in a 1930s Ford rumble seat; he soon decided that girls preferred a modern car like a Henry J.

More importantly, since Nan, David, Jerry and I lived out our teenage years in T.C., each of us had to find our own way spiritually. Mother and Dad were good examples of parents who loved the Lord and were obedient to their callings. Daily they both visited the congregants, giving encouragement and counsel; yet, none of us were given the wisdom and guidance given to the people—except for times of reproof. Yes, we did hear it in sermons, but our spiritual and emotional needs far exceeded that of the adults. Although we eventually understood that the disconnect with our parents and with each other was not intentional, the negative effect lasted far into our adult years. We had to search out for ourselves the life God intended for us.

Remembering Granddad's dramatic ministry, Dave saw beyond the sacrifices of the family to a life of adventure. The call to preach still burned within him since camp. Dad was proud to see his firstborn son deciding to follow in his footsteps. He kept Dave's zeal burning by taking time to instruct him how to prepare a sermon: "Study the Bible, pray, and then prepare a good outline."

Dave took Dad's advice and put it to work at an early age. When he was sixteen he felt ready to prove himself a preacher. He approached Dad with a proposition: "Dad, I think I'm ready to preach. Maybe I should preach in our church first. Then do you think you could line up a few speaking engagements in some of the nearby churches?"

"Son, you preach for me; then we'll talk about the other." Dad believed in a man proving himself first, even his own sons.

Eyebrows arched heavenward when Dad announced to the congregation that Dave would be preaching at the evening service. We drove to church that night with quaking hearts. Dave had Dad's big Bible in his hand and sat cool and collected. Dad seemed more nervous than any of us.

"Do you have your outline, Son?"

"Yes, Dad."

"Don't worry if your knees shake. Your first time, you're bound to be nervous."

"I'm not nervous, Dad."

"That's fine, Son."

That night at church, we sang, we prayed, and the ushers took the offering. At last, Dave's hour had come: "And now I'm happy to have my son, David, come and preach his first sermon. Your responsive amens will make it easier for him to preach."

With a firm step, Dave strode to Dad's place behind the pulpit. He opened the big Bible, laid it down in front of him and looked up over the sea of eyes anxiously waiting for the pastor's son to speak.

We waited and waited. Not a sound came forth. His mouth hadn't even opened. He stood there, stiff and speechless, completely bound by fear. It took several moments for Dad to realize Dave's predicament. Quickly he walked to Dave's side, turned to the congregation and said, "Join me in prayer."

We thought Dad intended either to pray the benediction or deliver the message himself. Instead, he placed his hands on Dave's head and in his fervent voice prayed: "Father, David is bound by fear, and the author of fear is Satan. In the name of Jesus, I rebuke this spirit of fear. Release him that he may speak forth your Word. Now, Son, preach," and Dad sat down in the front pew.

Dave's first sermon lasted all of fifteen minutes. No one remembered what he said, but we knew that he had won a victory over the fear of facing an audience. Who could have predicted that his victory over fear would enable Dave to preach to audiences larger than either Granddad or Dad had ever faced?

After this preaching debut, Dad secured preaching engagements for Dave among his minister friends. By the time Dave graduated from high school, he was anxious to enter full-time ministry.

"Not before you've had some Bible school training," Dad insisted. He remembered the wise advice of his own father.

Two years after Nan left to attend Bible school, David set off for the same school almost penniless, but with an opportunity to earn his way and the promise of ten dollars a week, plus love letters to ease his lonely hours from Gwen, his wife-to-be.

Dave decided that after the end of his first year he was ready to begin his ministry. "Dad," he said, "I think I'll get some field experience; then go back to school." Dad couldn't find fault with David's decision. He had been sure of himself at the end of one year of schooling, too.

"All right, Son, but find out from God in which field of labor you are most needed and suited."

David did just that and no one would believe him, especially not Mother. Even Dad, with his tolerant disposition, wondered what had gotten into his seemingly levelheaded son to choose ventriloquism and puppets as his method of preaching the Holy Word of God. "It's my father coming out in him, I guess," Dad said.

Mother let Dave know how she felt in no uncertain terms: "Dave, surely God has a better ministry for you than such childishness." Actually, when Mother met Dave's puppet, Red, she thought more along the lines of ventriloquism being a form of witchcraft, but she carefully withheld her opinions from Dave. Instead she headed for her prayer closet. We all knew the content of her prayers.

But already Dave had purchased the equipment he needed to go on tour for children's crusades. "Don't touch that suitcase," he warned me one day when I curiously eyed a few of the magical tricks he had laid out on the dining room table. When he poured a pitcher of milk into a rolled up newspaper, it disappeared; and a stick went limp when anyone else but Dave handled it. Don and I watched in awe as our big brother did tricks we had never been permitted to see at the amusement parks.

If it hadn't been for Mother's prayers, my brother Dave may have taken up an offer from a television station to soft-pedal the Gospel to children. No reports of his success changed her mind. She meant to "pray through" until her son came to his senses. When at last Dave came home with the news that he planned to be a candidate for a small church not too far from Pittsburgh, Mother began smiling again.

One crisis followed another in our household. Most of them were resolved through prayer and patience—and longsuffering! The worst crisis affecting all of us, and especially Mother, was my father's continuous bout with stomach ulcers. A thorough checkup in a Pittsburgh hospital revealed that Dad had several ulcers, which periodically caused bleeding and a great deal of pain. The doctor gave him some sound and stern advice: "Reverend, you need to relax. Why not take up golf or fishing?"

This second scare seemed to bring Dad to his senses. He was more relaxed around the house and even surprised us by taking the doctor's advice to heart. Dad had used his days in the hospital to reflect upon his past and that of his family.

Soon after, Dad shared his thoughts with me. He took a sheet of typing paper from his desk drawer and drew a large circle, dividing it into four equal parts. In each part he wrote a word in bold print: PLAY, FAMILY, CHURCH, STUDY. "This is the way it should be—a time for each. Up until now, I haven't lived like this. All my time is for the church and studying, and now I see the results in my body and in our family. I've had the wrong perspective on the life of sacrifice and I mean to make some adjustments."

Dad's resolve to make changes led him to the golf course and what a shock it was to the family, especially when we heard that

Mother had tried her hand at golfing, too. But the greatest change would be prompted by the words of John, Dad's brother.

When the spiritual energy of the church lagged, Dad felt the need of someone beside himself to energize the people. I especially remember the time he invited Uncle John and two other young men from a Texas Bible College to come for a week of preaching. They had organized a trio to represent their college and earn money for their tuition. Uncle John, second son born to Granddad Wilkerson and Maxine, did not look or act like his father but, he had the same charm and boldness of Granddad.

Dad had tried to build the congregation by initiating a door-to-door canvas of the town to seek out the non-churched people, but no one seemed bold enough to ask people if they believed in Christ as their Savior. Uncle John put everyone to shame with his evangelism skill in the downtown shoe shop. He bought a pair of shoes in exchange for a promise that the clerk selling the shoes would come to hear his trio sing and preach. Much to everyone's surprise, the young man attended and brought his brother. Eventually he joined the church and Dad preformed his marriage to one of the young women of our congregation.

Uncle John not only caused a stir within the congregation, he also stirred Dad to think about his future ministry. After hearing of the struggles of building and constant financial stress, he looked Dad in the eye and said, "Kenneth, why do you keep on struggling here. You are capable of a greater ministry than here in Turtle Creek."

His remark angered Mother; she felt it reflected on Dad's ability to be a pastor. Dad needed to hear an honest observation. He had faithfully and diligently worked to build both a building and a congregation; yet it seemed that the membership would never grow in proportion to the sacrifices made. He concluded that he had planted the seeds and now another man would be needed to "water the soil and reap the fruit."

It took months of soul searching before Dad took action.

Once again, he would be required to place his name with congregations seeking a pastor. He hated the competitive procedure of being a candidate among two or three other ministers. He remarked in jest that he could not sing, play the piano, or dance—we all knew he meant it would be difficult to compete with a new generation of ministers who were not necessarily known for their preaching skills. Many churches were looking for high profile men who had more talents than preaching and being a shepherd.

I was unprepared for Dad's decision to "try out" in churches and totally shocked when he announced that the Scranton Assembly had voted him as their pastor. Like Nan, I found the denominational Bible school lacking in instruction in the career I had chosen as a teacher. With Dad's encouragement, I had applied for a scholarship, and to my delight I received a four-year scholarship to the University of Pittsburgh. I would need financial support from my parents along with a part-time job. I firmly stuck to my goal until the day Dad announced he had been voted as the pastor of the Scranton Assembly.

There were no offers of money or encouragement from my parents. All my dreams of becoming an educator rapidly dispersed before my eyes. Despite my efforts to remain in T.C., it became impossible to take advantage of the scholarship. I was disappointed that my dreams had no weight of importance in my parents' eyes because I had chosen a secular career. It seemed as if I was forced to stand back while someone else took control of my future. I found comfort and guidance in the words of Jesus: "But seek first the kingdom of God, and his righteousness; and all these things shall be added unto you." I chose to believe God would add "something" else in place of the scholarship.

Mother and Dad seemed energized by the prospects of moving out of T.C. and into a well-established church. Don was apprehensive of attending a new high school, and I, with no dream to carry with me, sadly joined in the horrendous job of packing up eleven years of accumulation. But for Mother and Dad it meant being relieved of many burdens that had taken a heavy toll upon Dad's body. He seemed excited about a new challenge and pleased about more favorable amenities. A parsonage, a new automatic washer and dryer, a full-time custodian who also took care of the parsonage needs, and a raise, all boosted his morale. The "bitter medicine" given to Dad by Uncle John had turned out to be just what the doctor ordered!

## CHAPTER 13

# THE FINAL JOURNEY

In our move to Scranton in 1956, the Holy Spirit's involvement in the affairs of our family became apparent to all of us. During those years, we were taken to mountain top experiences and guided through the valley of death. We were able to rejoice through the darkest of days because God was present to sustain us, just as He had been for all the generations of the Wilkerson family.

The Scranton Assembly's history had seen our denomination's finest pastors in its long history. Dad felt greatly honored to follow in the footsteps of these esteemed brethren. The new challenge energized his weary body even though he understood another building program faced him. He loved the new flock of "sheep" from the very beginning and they wholeheartedly responded to Dad's ministry.

Right off, he instituted his musical trademark—chorus time, interspersed with testimonies—and the congregation loved the audience participation. One of the older members reported to another member, "Our new pastor has brought a bit of heaven to us. We haven't sung like that in years; it's like the days of the old-time religion." Like he had always done, he took the spiritual temperature of the congregation by the testimonies of victories and thanksgiving to the Lord.

Sometimes he also discovered dissensions brewing—like the

time an older man stood up to thank the Lord that he did not have the "devil's box" in his home. Dad stopped right then to expound on what may be wrong for one member may not be wrong for another: "Owning a television," he explained, "must be a personal decision, not a matter to discuss in the congregation."

TV had been equally divisive in our own home. In T.C., David brought the first television into our house. Mother did not approve and had it banished to an attic bedroom. In Scranton, she finally gave in to Dad's insistence that it was not a sin and brought a small television for their bedroom. In later years, Mother purchased her own and gave it living room status in her apartment.

Dad believed that there were two subjects that should be preached periodically: one on the command and rewards of tithing, and the other about Christ's return for the Church and the believer's eternal rewards in heaven. He believed heaven to be a real place, and he portrayed our days on earth as a short passage in time when each person is given the choice to be reborn and to offer his or her life to the Lord and to continue His work on earth. The time of preparation for eternity would be climaxed with a trip through space to a city whose streets are paved with gold, where mansions stand among Eden-like gardens and where Satan can never harm us.

He would tell the congregation: "Don't think you'll be sitting on a soft cloud playing a harp. Heaven will be a busy place, its capitol the heavenly Jerusalem. Talk about the wonders of inter-planetary travel—we'll be the people traveling all over this universe! No longer will our knowledge be limited; God Himself will reveal His mysteries. And don't be surprised when you meet Kenneth Wilkerson playing a violin. That's been one of my great desires. I haven't achieved it here, but in heaven I'll be an accomplished violinist!" Dad's enthusiasm caught our attention. I, for one, lost my fear of death and heaven.

Tithing ten percent of his income was not an option for our parents. In our father's sermons on the subject of tithing, we were taught about the ancient Hebrew customs of tithing commanded by God. In the Barnesboro days, our "fruit cellar" was filled with the farmers' tithes on their vegetables, fruits and jellies. Dad believed God would bless people who tithed and enable them to give offerings above ten percent. He was not embarrassed to tell people to expect God to bless them with some kind of increase because they honored God with what He had provided. Dad taught us not to strive for or ask for prosperity, but he did believe the Bible taught that our needs would be supplied according to our faith and our obedience to spiritual laws.

Tithing and creating special funds to help needy people was and is still common practice in our family. Dad kept a portion of his tithe in a secret compartment in his wallet. This money was reserved for the needs of pastors or missionaries. We remember Dad telling Mother to leave the grocery money home when a missionary was the guest speaker at the church—he knew she would want to share the budgeted money and there would not be enough for food. Mother soon learned creative ways to save a small portion of the budget and hid her "savings" in books and in her sewing boxes, secretly giving to people as she was led by the Spirit to do so. We have all learned if we "cast our bread upon the waters," it will return to meet our needs—often in very unusual ways. Although we were never taught to seek to be prosperous or pray for prosperity, we were shown the examples in the Scriptures of God blessing people because of their obedience to His commands. And we learned from our mother how to save our own special cache for missions.

With each building program, Dad would stress tithing was to be separate from offerings for the new church. To emphasize the separation, he encouraged people to save their offerings in a special container and place it in a prominent place in their kitchen. In Scranton, he had them bring their offerings and empty them into a wheelbarrow. It would be wheeled to the altar, dedicated to the Lord for use in the new church, and put in the bank the next day.

Dad liked to brag about his congregation. He wrote to his friend Gillam, "My people love the Word of God. They've been fed the choicest meat of the Scriptures. I really have to dig deep for new thoughts. There's no difficulty preaching to them; they sit there drinking it in as fast as I can preach it."

Dad spent many hours in his study preparing new sermons that would build their faith and their commitment to Christ and the Church. Soon they would need to launch out into a building program. Dad prayed for unity, recognizing it could only happen when people were obedient to the Word of God.

I wish all five of us would have had the benefit of living in the Scranton days and being part of a loving and vibrant congregation. After one year at a Bible Institute, Nan moved to Washington, D.C., to find government office work. She shocked us all with her announcement that she had married a Catholic. David married his church sweetheart, Gwen, and introduced her to the joys and hardships of building up a small town church. Jerry also married a girl from the T.C. church and remained in the area working in the grocery business. Only Don and I were able to enjoy a congregation who greeted our family with open arms and treated us with love and respect. But we were not destined to enjoy the warmth and care of a loving and more prosperous congregation for very long.

God revealed my destiny to my father, who noticed that I had been making nightly visits to the church to pray. And so, one February evening I did not think it strange to hear my father announce at the dinner table, "Ruth, I've been praying today concerning your future, and God told me you'll be meeting the man who'll be your husband in the very near future."

"Well, that sounds better than my plans to teach in Alaska," I retorted with a laugh.

Dad was serious, that I knew; he never joked about receiving a message from God. But I was young and it did sound a little preposterous. Most of my heart wanted to believe his startling revelation, but part of me doubted it could happen as spectacularly as it had for women in the Christian novels.

In April, a young man who had been in training for the Catholic priesthood visited our church during a revival series. He had been coaxed into coming by one of his aunts who had recently joined our church. Kye had been miraculously healed in an Oral Robert's healing service and was told to find a Spirit-filled church to attend. She immediately asked the congregation to pray for her unsaved nephew, Don.

With much pleading and many tears, his aunt persuaded Don to attend a revival at our church. I unofficially met Don when I sat behind him in church during the April revival. When he laughed out loud at the evangelist's opinion that "holy water" was no more holy than tap water, I knew he was not married to the Catholic Church. I also heard the inner voice of the Spirit saying to me, "Ruth, this is the man you will marry."

Of course, I was shocked and delighted. I had absolutely no doubt that my father's prediction was about to come true. After work the next day, I rushed to the hospital where Dad was recuperating from a delicate operation to remove part of his ulcerated stomach, and I told him my good news. Even though he was weak and in pain, Dad sat straight up in bed and, with a huge smile on his face, made another prediction: "Ruth, if this is the man God has chosen to be your husband, it will all work out for good." We were both amazed and pleased of how lovingly God had responded to our prayers about my future.

My father's confidence and assurance that God was involved in my future, gave me the courage to respond positively to Don's aggressive pursuit. When Don presented himself at the altar to pray the sinner's prayer, I had no questions as to whether or not Don was the man God had chosen for me to marry. Within a month we were engaged!

In that same cold winter of 1958, I came home from work to find Dad and Mother in a state of consternation. Dad had a New York City newspaper spread out on the kitchen table and there, staring out from the front page was a picture of son number one looking like a frightened small-town preacher trying to confront the evils of a wicked city with a large, black Bible. The story of David breaking into a court in session read like a bizarre story that could only happen in some other family—never ours!

Dad shook his head in shock of what he read. "What's gotten into David? He's just like my father—one spectacular project after another. And now this! I wonder what he was thinking."

David had not yet shared his secret closet, prayer experiences with Dad. It looked like one more of David's creative ideas for preaching the Gospel—only this one became very public!

We learned the story of what had happened when David stopped by the parsonage on his way home from the city. Dad wanted to hear his story from the beginning. He had to know what prompted David to make a public fool of himself, stirring up anger among ministers in two of our denomination's districts.

Sitting around the kitchen table, David poured out his heart starting with the restlessness he had felt for months and the conviction that he should sell his television and give his time to prayer and fasting. Mother and Dad understood the spiritual stirrings causing David to draw apart from the world to pray. They were not surprised at the depth of anguish David felt looking at the drawing in Life magazine of seven young boys on trial for the murder of a paraplegic. They were not even shocked to hear him say the Holy Spirit had instructed him to help the boys on trial. But they were stunned by the dramatic manner in which David chose to talk with them.

In the Pentecostal church, the Holy Spirit is not a questionable theological term to be ignored; He is the Spirit of Christ, a living Person who lives in every believer and communicates His will and purposes. We were taught we must live in obedience to the written Word of Christ so that we would be tuned to the "still, small voice" of His Spirit. Going before the judge in that New York courtroom was the boldest step of obedience David had ever taken.

The newspaper account of David interrupting the court in his effort to approach the judge and seek permission to visit with the boys, read like a Hollywood drama—the kind that portrays preachers as being naïve and ignorant. The photo of a scared young man holding up a large Bible accompanying the story added to the drama of an already sensational story. David's shock of the outcome of what he thought was a mission directed by the Spirit, left him drained of reasons for his actions and humbled by his failure to get permission to visit the seven boys on trial.

When David finished giving his account, Dad replied as only a concerned father would: "I only hope I'm respected enough to be able to save you from losing your ordination. There have been a lot of complaints, David, and I can't say that I blame them. You need to put more thought into your actions." Dad's peers had elected our father as Assistant Superintendent of the Pennsylvania District; he hoped he could convince them to take a "wait and see" attitude.

After the initial shock of David's courtroom drama and Dad's many calls to church leaders urging them to act carefully in their assessment of what they believed to be nothing more than an embarrassment to our denomination, we thought the episode was behind us. Not for David! He believed the call had come to him from God and he meant to obey.

Dad and Mother began to understand the seriousness of David's commitment to the call from the many visits he made to New York. In July of 1958, my fiancé Don and I, along with my brother Don, decided to travel to New York and see for ourselves the new venture of our visionary brother. Not one of us had been to the "big city." We weren't even sure we could find our way, and we worried about getting mugged or having our car stolen. In the end, our curiosity overruled these fears.

Somehow we found our way to St. Nicolas arena, and with an uneasy feeling in the pit of our stomachs, we parked the car and rushed into the arena. As we stepped into the auditorium, all our fears subsided. Loud, joyful singing and clapping greeted us. Christians from the Assemblies of God Spanish churches in the city had joined with David in a two-week crusade to preach the Gospel to the gangs. I can still recall the powerful sounds of the hymn, "There is Power in the Blood," being sung in Spanish:

*Hay poder, poder—sin igual poder*
*En Jesus, quien murio;*
*Hay poder, poder—sin igual poder*
*En la sangre que El vertio*

The three of us looked at each other and smiled. Something powerful could be felt in the arena—a power we had never felt before. We joined the singing in English:

*There is pow'r, pow'r, wonder-working pow'r*
*In the Blood of the Lamb; There is pow'r, pow'r,*
*Wonder-working pow'r, in the precious Blood of the Lamb.*

That night, we saw the power of Christ changing the hearts and minds of gang members who had come to the arena as we had, out of curiosity. We would learn later that Nicky Cruz, a violent gang leader destined to follow in David's footsteps, was among them. For me, it was the beginning of my adult realization of the victory Christ had died for, and a short exposure to a world I had not seen or heard about. The full impact of the Cross and the Resurrection was yet to be understood before I could believe for the freedom of people living in slavery to addictions.

No one in that auditorium, not even David, understood God's plans for the sixties generation and the generations to come, and neither could they have imagined how God purposed to use unknown and very ordinary men and women to accomplish His plans. My brother seemed to be the person least likely to lay the foundation for a worldwide ministry to gangs and addicts. The family listened, watched and prayed as the vision unfolded. Mother and brother Don also had no clue they would become part of such a ministry.

My father knew well the importance of being led by God. He had experienced the hardships of making decisions without consulting God, and he knew the joy of success when he trusted God to guide his steps. He could look out the parsonage window and see a monument to his victories. In the place where once stood a stately but old and antiquated stone church, a large, brick colonial church with its steeple rising high in the heavens spoke of God's faithfulness to Dad. No, Dad could not deny his son's vision. He had had visions, too, of a different nature, but no less and no more visionary than David's. I knew my father well enough to say he prayed that God would help David see his vision through.

For Dad, the vision for the Scranton church had been his crowning joy. He took over the pastorate not long after the Board had voted to add to their present sanctuary. The parsonage had been moved to the corner lot to make room for a new addition, but Dad had a greater vision for the church. He wanted to tear down the old church and build a new sanctuary. And he needed to convince the congregation—never an easy task.

He used the same faith-building sermons that he had preached in T.C. to inspire the people to choose a different plan for the church building. As usual, he had a few stubborn "mules" but Dad travailed with the faithless and inspired those of faith to claim the promises of God. Borrowing a story from the teaching of Jesus on the dangers of attaching a new garment to an old one, and the foolishness of pouring new wine into old wineskins, Dad gave the congregation many reasons why the old building had to come down. He preached until the congregation had a mind to build.

Within a year, the old stone church was demolished to make room for the new sanctuary that had been unanimously accepted—but not without struggles. The congregation had to temporarily relocate and Dad worried about loss of the fringe group of people who had not yet made a commitment to the Church. Plus, there were countless changes in the building plans to suit the city. Worse, it all came to a standstill when the unions protested the use of non-union workers. Nevertheless, two years later, dedication day became a time to celebrate many victories. Even the doubters bragged, "Look what we've done!"

The spirit of revival reigned in our beautiful, new church. Dad's vision beheld a growing and prosperous church. Good things began to happen. The town suddenly seemed aware of a group of vibrant Pentecostals in their midst. My father was invited to speak at a Presbyterian church to explain the significance of the Holy Spirit coming on the day of Pentecost.

After meeting Don in the sanctuary of the new church, we were married four months later. My brother, Don, preached his first sermon from its pulpit. And it was one of the first churches to hear of David's new ministry to New York City gangs and drug addicts. The move to Scranton had proved to be what Dad had hoped and prayed for in his last stressful year in T.C.

But on my visits home I noticed Dad's physical strength ebbing, and much worse, his spirit seemed so low my heart was distressed. "Something is wrong with my father," I repeatedly told my husband. Dad had had a serious operation just before I met Don and two-thirds of his stomach had been removed because of bleeding ulcers. We naturally thought he had not fully recuperated. It is a thrill to have the unknown revealed by the Holy Spirit before the event actually happens. It is not an unusual occurrence to those who have had the spiritual experience of being led by the Spirit. Yet, God in His compassion kept the knowledge of our father's slow death from us, even though so many tragic signs pointed toward it.

A year after his operation, Dad had gone visiting. Driving home, a car banged into his rear bumper as he paused for a stop sign. It was a hard hit jolting Dad badly enough to cause him pain for several months. The pain developed into severe headaches that brought on an unbalanced walk and the loss of the ability to focus his eyes. His doctor sent him to the hospital for X-rays, but nothing seemed to be wrong. However, his blood pressure was so dangerously high the doctor issued an ultimatum: "If you want to live, you must give up the ministry. Retire now and you'll add ten years to your life."

Only Mother and Dad shared this news, both feeling that God could continue to strengthen Dad for the work he had been called to do. But the answer to Dad's prayer for strength was not forthcoming. The headaches became so severe the family doctor recommended an examination by a neurologist. The result of this examination was tragic news. Dad had a clot in one of his neck arteries. He was given two choices: to have an operation with a risk of death or immediately retire. Dad made his decision in the doctor's office: "Doctor, I'd rather die in the pulpit than retire or live the rest of my days in a wheelchair."

I wanted to talk to my father about my concerns, but he seemed to be lost in a fog of despair, not wanting to talk, not wanting to read, and not having his morning prayers. "God, how can this be?" I questioned God constantly. I wondered if Mother noticed Dad's behavior. I could not bring myself to ask her, but I could tell by the sadness of her face she had a serious concern for my father's state of mind and health.

Then at last I had my opportunity. Dad asked me to drive him into a nearby town for an appointment with his ophthalmologist. On the way, he talked of his struggles: "Ruth, I guess you've noticed I haven't been winning many victories lately. I don't know why I went through this dryness of my soul. But I can tell you this—I've come through it with a new and greater vision of the Lord. The dark veil over my mind and spirit has been lifted and I feel on the verge of a great victory."

The following Sunday the subject of Dad's sermon was the return of Christ for His Church. He expressed his personal thoughts: "I'm looking forward to the day Jesus comes in the clouds to take His Bride (the Church) home. I see Jesus waiting for the Father to say, 'Now, my Son, bring home those you have gathered for the Kingdom.' I see the Lord's arms stretched out to welcome me home." Dad lifted his arms and looked toward the heavens as if he really did see the Lord and said to the people, "I'm ready to go, are you?" His face glowed with peace and joy. We couldn't help notice he had won another victory. I glanced at Mother; tears were streaming down her cheeks. I thought, "Mother knows of Dad's victory, too."

Mother sensed something else. Dad had been close to death several times, and now she watched him suffer again, such suffering she had never seen before. She kept her fears to herself, only telling us part of Dad's difficulties in walking, in focusing his eyes, and not being able to think clearly. She wondered what kind of victory God had prepared for His servant.

Dad did seem to get a little better. He wanted to talk to my husband and me about plans to enter the ministry, he enjoyed my younger brother's weekend visits from Bible college, he talked about setting Jerry up in a small business in Scranton which meant parting with some of their savings. Phone calls from David reporting on his ministry to the gangs never ceased to amaze Dad—he invited David to tell his story to the congregation and hoped they would financially support his son's ministry. His thoughts seemed to be focused on the future of his children. None of us realized we were about to lose our father.

He wrote his friend, Gillam: "I don't seem to be able to hit those keys very well…that's been one of my problems since the accident…I can still shout the victory, and preach all over the church. And I can hold on to the pulpit and sing like an angel from heaven when I am anointed. I love fellowship, and this year has been hard on me—the children have been here, but I miss my buddy."

True friend that he was, Gillam came to Scranton a week later. Several years later when I began gathering stories of our family's history, Gillam wrote about his visit with Dad that week:

*We visited together in the study. He told me about his hospital stay, all his trials during his sickness and the accident that had caused it all. He told me that when he was in the hospital for those weeks with only four walls to look at, his life seemed to him to be just one trouble after another. His body was not up to it. He prayed to die. This shocked me. One day the doctor came in and he asked him if he could go home. The doctor replied that he could see no reason why not, if he really wanted to go. Kenneth got the ball rolling and he went home. It was then that he wrote me. I replied that I could probably arrange to come over later in the spring. I think he called when he received my answer and asked me to come. This was quite sudden, but I felt I should arrange it and I did. He told me, "Now that I am home, things look good to me. I look at everything, every stick of furniture. It all looks good to me and I want to live." I took him to a doctor who, it was said, could help the severe pain in his head. He advised him not to have the nerve cut in his neck. Kenneth had already vetoed this idea. While I was with him, it became real to me how hurt he had been with the loss of equilibrium. He took hold of my arm as we walked, he took hold of the pews as he went down the church aisle and he held on to the pulpit when he talked. All this was noticeable, but I had no idea that it was serious.*

In answer to my question of what Dad had told him about David's ministry in New York City, Gillian wrote:

*Concerning his estimate of Dave's activities, it was generally one that reflected what he saw in Dave that neither Dave nor anyone else for that matter knew at the time. Whenever he heard of anything that Dave had done that was unusual, he was always quick to say,*

*"Just like Dad!" This meant there had shown up in Dave some of the genes that were evidently generously imparted to his granddad: J.A. Wilkerson. Kenneth never was surprised at anything he heard, but rather, I would say, enjoyed it with that thrill that any parent would have who had raised a child for God. The thrill contained an element of wonder in it. That Dave would come up with some of his enterprises and carry them off was to him nothing short of amazing. And to think that his dad, in a sense, lived again in Dave was also something he pondered often. Both he and I felt that Granddad Wilkerson never reached the potential of which he was capable. And, no doubt, it was to him an evidence of God's goodness that Dave was chosen to reach the destiny that Granddad abrogated because of his willful ways.*

*The visit was too brief but I had to get back. When I said good-bye, I thought he looked unusually well. Though it took him quite a while to get downstairs, he looked good.*

Just three days after Gillam left, Mother called our apartment early in the morning and calmly said, "Ruth, I'm waiting for an ambulance. The doctor seems to think Dad has a virus, but I feel it is much worse."

I hung up the phone with a sense of foreboding and went into the living room and knelt to pray, but I could only weep. I heard the still, small voice of the Holy Spirit so clearly in my mind: "Ruth, your father is not going to live. It's time for him to go home." I had not experienced the awfulness of final separation from someone I loved, and neither could I comprehend the finality of physical death.

Two days later, on his way to work, my husband stopped at the hospital to check on Dad's condition. Just minutes after his arrival, he called the parsonage where we were staying with Mother: "Ruth, I was with your father when he died—he went peacefully." Instantly I experienced the deep sadness of knowing I'd never see my father until I went home to heaven. Who would keep our family together since we were already fragmented? What would happen to Mother, and my brother Don, and my husband and me? What would happen to the church?

I had so many perplexing questions and no answers. During the Sunday morning worship service, I sat on the baptistery steps hoping to be comforted by the hymns and prayers without having to be in the sanctuary. I could not make sense of Dad's death; he was only fifty-four and he had many dreams yet unfulfilled. The family still needed his guidance, and prayers, and words of encouragement. The church needed his leadership.

While the people prayed, I cried out to God to show me why He had allowed my father to die at so early an age. I flipped open my Bible and my eyes were drawn to Isaiah 57:1,2. I read aloud: "The righteous perisheth, and no man layeth it to heart; and merciful men are taken away, none considering that the righteous is taken away from the evil to come. He shall enter into peace..." (KJV).

The words of Isaiah assured me that God had taken Dad because of His love for him—God knew he could not endure what lay ahead. I accepted this as words of comfort, knowing my father's physical condition and his prayer to be taken home to heaven rather than facing a life without being able to preach.

The shock of our father's death settled over the family and the church like a cloud of darkness. Friends and family helped us to find our way through the funeral. A happy event of my childhood years seemed to be playing out again when Granddad and Maxine, and Aunt Elaine, and Uncles John, Gordan, and Paul stepped into the parsonage. And true friend that he had always been to Dad, Gillam returned to be with the family. In the midst of our grief they brought the joy of family that we all needed.

At the funeral home, crowded with family and friends, Granddad made the gathering a revival. He greeted the mourners and then proceeded to give his personal testimony of salvation and healing to an audience whom he knew hadn't heard his story. Yes, he lifted his leg as high as he could in his "young age" of seventy-seven. If my father was watching from heaven, I am sure he had a smile on his face and said, "Preach it, Dad." That would be the last dramatized sermon we would hear from Granddad. He would join Dad in heaven three years later.

In spite of my sorrow I could not forget the most wonderful part of death that Dad had believed: that the resurrection life of Christ in him would raise him up from death to live forever with the Lord. Although he would physically die, Dad believed his spirit would immediately be with the Lord, and in heaven he would be given a new body. That was Dad's faith—and he was confident God would honor his faith. I know where my father is right now and I know that I will see him when it is my time to go home to be with the Lord. I'll look for Dad in the heavenly orchestra—he'll be in the string section!

## CHAPTER 14

# BLAZING NEW PATHS

No one in our family could have imagined the changes about to take place after our father's death. Nothing would be the same; everything would change for Mother, for Don and David, and for my husband and me. We would travel down new and very different paths. We would each face great struggles and great victories. Had God shown us these paths in advance and the battles we would fight, no doubt we would have asked Him to remove the "cup of sorrow" from us. At the same time, had God shown us the victories and the spoils to be reaped, we would have gladly said, "Thy will be done." The path we each took would call for faith in the God of our Fathers.

Suddenly, for Mother, life meant going on without Dad, to where, she did not know. She was not prepared for a job in the secular workforce. In Scranton she had been ordained into ministry since she often had to fill Dad's place in the pulpit because of his many bouts with stomach ulcers. But she did not enjoy standing before a congregation to preach. Fortunately, about a year before Dad died, Mother shocked us with her first license to drive, especially since her first attempt to drive almost ended in a disaster. Mother's destiny seemed settled when the church Administrative Board approached her about continuing Dad's work as their pastor. This was not often done in the Pentecostal churches, although there were many women missionaries and evangelists, but the Board thought it would be good for the church and for Mother. My brother Don would be graduating from college in May and Mother believed that, with his help, she might be able to pastor the church. Reluctantly, and with many reservations about her qualifications and her desire for such a ministry, Mother agreed. There seemed to be no other path for her to choose.

Before his death, Dad had planned a revival crusade that would directly influence the path my husband and I would take. During the evangelist's time with us, we shared with him that my husband did not have someone to recommend him to a church needing a pastor. He immediately volunteered to introduce him to a District Presbyter in North Carolina where pastors were needed in the smaller churches.

Needless to say, my face dropped and I groaned when Don asked—rather told me we would be moving far from home, all the way to North Carolina. I did not want to go, but I had been well-versed in the teaching that women should submit to their husbands in ministry decisions. Since my father had planned the revival, I took it as a sign God had orchestrated our destiny and somehow He would help us to fulfill this mission and also take care of Mother after we were gone.

My brother had planned to assist Mother, but while he was still at school, David had written Don a letter and then followed it up with a phone call hoping to convince him to give serious thought to the ministry to gangs and addicts. Later on, when people would ask Don how he had received a call to the Teen Challenge ministry, Don, in his typical dry humor would laughingly reply, "It came by telephone."

He defends the manner by which his call came with a serious explanation of the day David called him at the Bible college dorm asking him to consider the streets of New York as his pulpit. Don was shocked and pleased that his brother asked for his help in the street ministry, even though he had neither a burden nor was he street-smart. But then, David had not been trained in street evangelism either.

David followed up the phone call with a letter giving Don an account of his vision for a great in-gathering of troubled youth into the Kingdom of God. David's compelling plea for people like Don, who were dedicated to God and the command of Christ to go into the streets of the city and preach the Gospel, could not be ignored.

Don was torn between Mother's need for his assistance at the church and David's plea for help in a new ministry—one for which Don had not been trained. In fact, he had never considered street evangelism to be his calling. Mother also called Don with a question he had been wrestling with for weeks: "Are you going to New York to join Dave?"

She had also been wrestling with questions of her own: could she cope with all the responsibilities of being a pastor? Should she take David's offer to join him in New York? These were difficult decisions for Don and Mother to resolve; they were torn between two very different kinds of ministries. Mother admitted she could not cope with all the problems of being a pastor. Don was excited about helping David, but very apprehensive about street ministry with gangs. David had been praying for partners and who could be best counted on to be faithful and prayerful than his own mother and brother! Much prayer and many discussions between Mother, David, and Don helped them to come to an agreement that together they would forge into unfamiliar territory and trust God to guide them.

In the winter of 1960, the Teen Age Evangelism ministry had been officially formed with the help of Assemblies of God ministers in New York City. They began with a zero balance in the treasury, but with an abundance of faith in God to provide for the establishment of the ministry to youth in their city. Shortly after this memorable meeting, David established an office in a three-room office at Victory Boulevard on Staten Island, almost two years from his first trip to the City—and in the same month our father went to be with the Lord. An inner room furnished with a desk, a sofa, and a hot plate doubled as a home for David.

In July, a month after my husband and I left for the Deep South, Mother moved to Staten Island with just enough furniture for a small apartment. David had invited her to join him as a kind of "Girl Friday"—as she called herself. She faced having to adjust to a different life style: she was back to apartment dwelling; she had to learn to deal with a variety of cultures and languages; and she had to brush up on her long forgotten secretarial skills. Her worst fear was driving on the busy streets. As if that wasn't enough to cope with, David could not promise her a salary—at least not until the bank balance began to grow. Mother thought she could handle all these changes, but it worried her that she might be a liability for David, rather than an asset.

After Don's first experience as a church evangelist, he joined Mother and David in the Staten Island office. He relieved Mother of her mailroom and post office duties and took over the many trips to the store for glue and string, and other simple office supplies. They both put in hours sending out literature requested by local churches that David had written and published, specifically geared for a generation with problems not previously addressed.

To Don, a newly ordained minister working as a mail clerk did not look much like a ministry, but he liked sorting through the mail for donations so that he could rush off to the bank to cash a check for food to eat that night. It wasn't easy for Mother, either. Not even the therapeutic hours of work kept her from being aware of the birth pangs of the new and almost destitute ministry.

When enough money had accumulated, David wanted to make a movie to show in churches. He believed that congregations needed a visual picture of the drug culture to move their hearts to help save a lost generation. He wanted a graphic depiction of the horrors of drug addiction, so he asked a former addict to arrange a filming of a drug party on a Brooklyn rooftop where drugs were being shot into veins with hypodermic needles.

David poised his camera and took pictures of the youngsters heating heroin to liquefy it and then fill needles to inject themselves. Don held the lights steady, and just as one of the addicts plunged the needle into his arm, David fainted. This humbling experience, one among many, taught them that God would use their weakness to show Himself strong.

Don took the crude film they had titled, *Teen Age Drug Addiction*, on tour to churches on the East coast from New York to Florida. Months of traveling, staying in homes of strangers, and having to fend for himself for the first time, plus having to put aside his own dreams of being a pastor, all pressed in on Don.

Despite the success of gathering a host of supporters, Don returned to Staten Island feeling he had missed his calling. He unburdened his heart to David and received the advice he had hoped to hear. Soon Don was headed north to Vermont where his bride to be had been waiting anxiously for him to come and finalize their wedding plans. There he would encounter far worse trials than he had experienced traveling from church to church. Without job training, he was unable to secure positions to adequately provide for his new bride and himself. The small congregation of mostly older people gave no promises of future growth; and much worse, Cindy and he experienced the grief of a stillborn child.

David had his own struggles. There seemed to be no way to realize his dream for a home where he could invite the street gangs and addicts for spiritual training and shelter from their violent environment. He had the vision of the need, but not the finances to make it happen. Frustration led to relying on the traditional ways of evangelism—they were familiar to David and to people willing to support a ministry to youth.

David, with the help of pastors and youth from many

churches, worked long hours in a literature blitz hoping to reach thousands of teens on the streets of the city. At the end of three months they could only point to a handful of boys and girls who had been truly changed. They had sent youth out to bring in a huge harvest with only sickles in their hands. David realized literature distribution alone could not do the job.

A television program especially designed to capture a teenage audience proved to be successful, but very costly. David felt an uneasiness about continuing down that road. His heart was being drawn back to having personal contact with youth on the street. So each morning, David left his office and went back on the streets to talk face-to-face with gang members and drug addicts. Mother kept up her secretarial duties and she did a lot of praying.

One day, on a subway trip to Brooklyn, an idea seemed to leap into David's mind. David's imagination envisioned a home in the heart of the roughest part of the city. He already had decided to use the name given to the television series. The name, Teen Challenge Center, seemed a perfect fit for a permanent place to bring street youth who had responded to the Gospel.

In 1962, a series of financial miracles provided a four-story, red brick Georgian house at 416 Clinton Avenue in Brooklyn— the first among many residents for youth who would be reaped from the streets of New York City and beyond.

While David had his miracles, Don doggedly kept working on his quest for maturity in the pastoral ministry, until he received a letter from David who wrote: "Don, the work has grown tremendously in the past several months and I need your assistance. I need someone I can completely trust and depend upon. It won't be easy for you and Cindy, but the challenge is here waiting for you to accept."

Accepting the challenge did not come easy for Don or Cindy. I recall receiving a letter in North Carolina from my brother asking for my advice and prayer. After reading about the seemingly losing battles to provide food for the table, and to realize any significant growth in the church, I answered his letter and questioned why he was hesitant in returning to New York. I believed he was better prepared to face the ministry in New York, and I encouraged him to accept.

A telephone call to Mother helped Don make the right decision. He asked her a direct question: "Does Dave really need me?" Her "yes" answer settled the confusion in his mind. It was at the new home of Teen Challenge, that Don and Cindy received a warm welcome from David and Mother. In spite of the small salary and having to move in with Mother who still maintained her apartment on Staten Island, Don felt better prepared to be a partner with David, and to take on his first assignment.

CHAPTER 15

# PARTNERS IN TEEN CHALLENGE

Our younger brother's preparation for a partnership with David in street ministry began in our home in Barnesboro. At an early age, Don received unique training especially designed by his siblings. He had the devoted attention of two older brothers, who, by age and necessity, were his designated caregivers and mentors. In a large attic bedroom, David and Jerry taught Don to not be a crybaby, to keep a reasonably clean room, to mind his own business, to love sports and play fair in games, do his homework, and never tattle on them.

While his brothers kept an eye on Don, so did God. Don did not know this in the early attic days, but he soon heard about God's watchful eye from his father's sermons. We all heard a lot about God's plans and purposes for His children, and without being told directly by our parents, we knew we were included, and that we had one great mission in life: to discover for ourselves the plans God had for us and follow them. Don seemed able to focus on purpose and adventure. Maybe his view of God and dreams of doing exploits for God started way back in those attic days when he felt the love and protection of family.

In 1969, after several years of experience, doing "exploits" for God, Don wrote a book describing his first years in the street ministry. In the book, he confesses that carrying out God's vision for the generations of the sixties, given first to his brother and then to him, was not made easier because of the assurance this was God's plan for him.

He remembers the struggles well:

*As long as I had been allowed to do my preaching and witnessing in the church, I had been in my element...my ministry had been pulpit oriented. For me there was now a fear of stepping out of the pulpit and onto the street corner with the same ministry. This street ministry was so new, so different, so frightening that I could not cope with it at first. It was a very real fear, not of bodily harm, but a fear which, nevertheless, quickens the heartbeat to a jackhammer pace and which dries the throat* (The Gutter and the Ghetto, p. 28).

Our parents and visiting missionaries spoke of having a burden for the lost. Today, churches don't tend to use the term "burden" any longer. The modern word for burden is passion. A person passionate about his ministry is usually one who is zealous, enthused, energized, and earnest. I have been a witness to Don's unwavering faith in God and to his passion to bring people into the Kingdom of God. At an early age, he set his face toward God, and even though there were enticements toward living recklessly and irreverently, he never sold out his spiritual heritage. This was the younger brother David knew he could trust and who would trust God in the many problems he would face in the Teen Challenge ministry.

Don and Cindy moved into Mother's small apartment in Staten Island. Each day they commuted to work, sometimes by car, but often they used the same method as Mother had been using since she feared driving through heavy traffic. Don humorously described the long, tiring trip to the Center in Brooklyn as "the deluxe route." It began with a two-block walk to the bus stop, and then a ferry boat ride across the channel, a bone-crunching ride on two different subway trains, topped off with another short walk to the Center. It never was a fun trip, but it did give them time to talk about plans for the day. On these daily trips, Mother would ask questions hoping to go beyond the obvious needs of the ministry and discover what she could do for her sons through prayer and spiritual counsel.

While Mother and Cindy handled phone calls and various office needs, Don teamed up with Nicky Cruz to drive into the Williamsburg section of Brooklyn where gangs roamed the streets. Nicky could speak Spanish and he could speak to the heart of these boys. Not many years before, he had been hated and feared among gangs, now he had a powerful testimony of a changed heart and a new life. The same Spirit that had reached Nicky's heart, reached into the hearts of the boys as they listened to his compelling message. Some of them agreed to be taken to the Center to hear more. At the Center, Nicky invited them to the chapel for a simple Gospel message, insisting they first stash all weapons in a closet. Some of these same gang members would eventually be among the Center's first residents.

One of Don's summer assignments at Teen Challenge took him to a very different kind of pulpit than he was accustomed to, in a place that once had been off limits during his teenage years. Coney Island, a well-known amusement park, seemed a logical place to meet a constant stream of people who needed to hear the Gospel. Don was asked to establish a portable chapel near the boardwalk where thousands of people passed by each day during the summer months. A nearby amusement called The Devil's Pit, reminded him what they were up against. The bar owner across from the new Surfside Chapel predicted it would never last—it lasted three years.

In a background of grinding machinery and the laughter of thrills, Don and Cindy began serious encounters with hundreds of fun seekers. Each night, with a team of volunteers, they presented a simple program of Christian music and testimonies. Don would give a short sermon and invite people to come in to talk personally with the workers. Loud speakers carried their music and words far beyond the chapel walls and the curious were caught by something new and different. Person to person, they planted the Gospel in the hearts and minds of many people. Some were ready to believe, others walked away bored and unbelieving, others scoffed. Nevertheless, an evident harvest was reaped, the hidden harvest yet to be seen.

Within a short time, Don became aware that God had answered his prayers, and had removed the doubts and fears, and had given him a boldness to preach on the streets. Imagine Don's surprise and joy when he was able to teach people how to witness to gang members and addicts including the "professional" evangelists who soon learned their formulas were ineffective on the street people.

David wisely allowed Don to ease into the ministry before he asked him to move into the Teen Challenge Center and coordinate all of the evangelistic programs. Don and Cindy had no concept of how it would change their daily routine. At first, they liked the idea that they would have their own apartment at the Center after commuting from Staten Island. But living at the Center meant that there would be no escape from the work at Teen Challenge. Now life and ministry were inseparable. Its sounds and its problems, as well as those of the neighborhood, were with them constantly.

Don became so emotionally involved in the daily needs of the residents that he often forgot the time of day or the day of the month. His schedule started early and ended very late, sometimes into the early hours of the morning if an emergency occurred. When an addict took off or pounded at the door to be let in, it was Don who rushed to the door; and like a concerned parent, Don waited up with the boys who struggled with the pain of going off drugs "cold turkey"—without help of medication.

As Evangelism Director, Don's responsibilities covered a long range of programs to meet the spiritual needs of men at the Center and in street evangelism. In the first year, David was present to share in the spiritual and administrative work, but when it became evident that money needed to be raised to finance the programs, David decided to conduct crusades wherever people would listen to his pleas for prayer and finances for the New York programs. With David gone, Don had all the work and worries of the ministry.

Don speaks frankly of those hectic days: "My anxiety increased in direct proportion to the number of days Dave was away. I could feel the pressures pyramiding; the more I tried to dig in and hold my ground, the more I found myself sinking deeper into the quicksand of frustration."

On each of David's return trips to the Center, Don unburdened his problems to David, and together they prayed about the needs. Too soon, David would leave for yet another crusade, and the pressure of the immense needs of the addicts would weigh so heavily on Don that he could not sleep or eat. The harder he tried to resolve problems, the worse they seemed to get. Sometimes Don shouldered the blame for the chaos; sometimes it seemed the staff didn't carry the burdens like he hoped they would, but often the logical person to blame was his brother, who Don reasoned, had taken on the easier part of the ministry of traveling and raising money.

Word filtered back to David of his brother's discontent. Upon his return, he summoned Don into his office. David seemed to know he needed to share his own struggles to establish the ministry, but he also expressed anger with Don for sharing his frustrations with staff members.

They should have been able to work through their problems as two men equal in their standing with God, but back then, Don believed that David's difficulty in resolving relational problems with mutual understanding was a problem common to men of "profound faith and vision." Don put David on a spiritual pedestal, and David accepted the position as a man whom God had given a special mission. Don's unexpressed feelings would someday lead to David and Don separating on less than good terms. At that time, they settled for resolving issues at hand without resolving the relational problems. When David left for more crusades, he felt assured that all was well between them, and that Don would find ways to solve the Center's problems. That is not what happened.

Instead of getting better, things were getting worse. Finances at Teen Challenge were so low that they barely had money for the next meal. They were understaffed and overcrowded. And they hadn't found anyone who could cope with the female addicts. In addition to all that, Don had paperwork piled high on his desk. All through these critical months David was gone for longer and longer stretches—occasionally for a solid month—and conversations between them were reduced to long-distance telephone calls and infrequent face-to-face visits.

To make matters worse, food and sleep deprivation were taking their toll on Don's body. And his marriage, so often intruded upon by others, would not survive without time to express love and affection in acts of kindness or times of laughter. These seem like such simple acts that any sincere Christian could do; but Don, being so blinded by what he believed God, and David and others expected of him, could not imagine the simplicity of living what Jesus had taught and practiced.

Our parents had often talked about the need to "pray through." We came to understand the importance of crying out to God, which meant pouring out our heart and soul to the Lord until we were prepared to listen to what the Lord had to say. Don recognized there was only One who could truly help him.

Being pushed to the brink of giving up opened his eyes to what he had needed to do all along, so off to the prayer closet he headed. One desperate session with God became a turning point in the way Don thought and handled problems and in the way he regarded his marriage. What he had known all along, that the ministry was the responsibility of the Holy Spirit and not his,

Don was now able to put into practice. Relinquishing the ministry and his personal struggles to the Holy Spirit would become an ongoing spiritual lesson Don would need to practice many times.

We all knew the value of making prayer a daily priority. Our parents had taught us that we must never cut ourselves off from communing with God. God, we understood, would not abandon us, but our pride and our foolishness in depending on our own abilities could sever the very Spirit-life we needed to accomplish the missions He had called us to do. In many trials and tribulations, Don learned prayer must be the strong tether that bound him to God.

David and Don also taught the boys at the Center to freely express worship to God and cry out to God to help them "die" to their old ways. One of the men came up with a rather unusual, although apt way of calling the others to chapel. He would step out into the hall and loudly call out, "Let's go! It's medication time." Both my brothers have hundreds of fascinating stories of how prayer transformed the lives of young men and women who cried out to God for help in the chapel at the Brooklyn Center.

In response to people who think that Pentecostal people pray too loudly, Don explains, "It is not our intent to place a premium on noise. We simply believe that the most effective type of prayer is the most spontaneous and uninhibited kind." Crying out to God did not originate with our denomination; we learned from ancient people of the Bible who unashamedly cried out to God in times of trouble. In our household, we heard our parents praying and we learned to cry out to God at the altars of our church. It seemed a normal way to pray and a good "medication" to give addicts.

There were many times David and Don had to put "feet" to their prayers. The need for additional buildings, finances, and dedicated staff were ongoing prayer requests to God. Their faith would be greatly tested and their works judged by their productiveness. It required togetherness in faith and in works—faith in the promise of the Lord that the Holy Spirit would guide them and confirm their efforts with the buildings needed and the finances to pay for them.

Our father had explained with an illustration, what we could do when our limitations blurred the guidance of the Spirit. "Life is like a long hallway with many doors of opportunity. When we can't seem to hear the still, small voice of the Spirit, we are left with only one option—to try every door and trust the Holy Spirit to open the right one for us." We learned on our own that we also had to trust God to close doors that we forced open!

They began to try the doors. They pushed and pushed one on Staten Island and just when it was about to open, it slammed shut. Then they tried a door on Long Island and just when they thought it would open, the neighbors held a town meeting to oppose "that kind of people" in their neighborhood. Door after door refused to open.

They were perplexed. It seemed as if God was taking them through a wilderness of miles and miles of travels and months of searching and still they had not found a suitable place to build a new center. It was hard for them to understand why God had not answered their prayers. Then one day they walked down their own street to investigate a rumor that an apartment building might be for sale. They knocked on three doors just a few buildings from the Brooklyn Center, and all three opened! Of course, as usual they were broke, so they gathered everyone to the chapel to pray for a miracle. Within three weeks God had supplied the money and they were able to pay off the debts on the new properties in cash. They were witnesses to another miracle and even greater miracles lay not far ahead.

From the beginning of a ministry to male addicts, David and Don prayed for a door to open to establish a stable home for females and for God to supply someone with a concern for young women hooked on drugs. The need became very evident when a temporary home was set up across the street from the Teen Challenge Center for men. But it was not a desirable setup. Early in the ministry they had discovered that women succumbed more easily to the call of the outside world. They became upset by the slightest thing that went wrong, and most women had a harder time breaking their drug habit than did the men. Thus, it was imperative that they find a highly competent person to be their director.

While speaking in the state of Washington, David met John Benton and his wife Elsie who had worked with Youth for Christ. They enthusiastically accepted the challenge to minister to the female addicts. Along with Don, they knocked at doors and finally settled on a beautiful, 23-acre estate in Garrison, New York. It is now known as the Walter Hoving Home in honor of the former chairman of Tiffany and Co. Mr. Hoving was instrumental in securing funds from the W. Alton Jones Foundation to provide the down payment and a yearly grant of $15,000 to cover the life of the mortgage.

Whenever David or Don shared the story of Teen Challenge and told stories of young people delivered from additions or life styles of violence, they were always asked about Mother's role in their ministry. Some people assumed she remained behind the scenes as a secretary; others thought she prayed and counseled with the men and women seeking help at the Center. People were surprised to learn Mother held both titles, and she also had her own specialized ministry. In fact, I probably was the person most shocked and delighted when Don wrote a letter to me about her ministry in Greenwich Village.

You would have to know my mother as I did, to understand why I was so amazed. She was a woman of great faith but she had to deal with many fears. During the time she spent working with my brothers, she had immeasurable influence upon our entire family and the Teen Challenge ministry.

## CHAPTER 16

# MOTHER'S SECOND CALLING

Mother's two callings—one as a minister's wife and the other in the ministry of Teen Challenge with David and Don—could not have been more dissimilar. I believe she enjoyed her second calling more than her first. But you could not get her to admit that she felt emotionally relieved when she was released from the responsibilities and limitations of being a minister's wife and taking care of the needs of a sickly man, while having to raise five children on a limited income. She would tell you she tried to be faithful in all her roles. What she would not talk about was the constant emotional stress never resolved while she struggled to be faithful.

As a child, I witnessed her struggles with fear, not understanding why Mother would stand at the bathroom window, gasping for air. Years later, I learned that I had been witness to her panic attacks. Mother dreaded tunnels, elevators, and rooms without windows. Yet she endured them all without complaint and without ever seeking help to overcome these fears. These were the least of her worries; there were fears far more frightening.

Every spring and fall, evangelists stayed in our home for at least two weeks. Mother had never learned the niceties of being a hostess so these occasions were not happy times for her. As soon as my sister and I were old enough to help, she depended on us to set the table and help with serving the food. In home economic classes, Nan learned to correctly set a table and she insisted I follow her instructions. I remember an evangelist, an older man, taking my hands in his and telling me I was worth my weight in gold. I had no idea what he meant, but I did know gold cost a lot of money. Years later, I understood that he had recognized how much my mother relied on a third grader to help her be a good hostess. His compliment boosted my self-esteem when I felt inadequate and became a blessing I now pass on to children in many forms.

In her years in church ministry, there was no stopping Mother's fear of offending God. She ruled us with a stern look; we always knew when she was displeased by something we had said or done. I became very aware of her unfounded fear of God during my teenage years when Dad's brother, John, and his college trio were visiting our home. I had learned to bypass Mother's strict holiness rules by taking jewelry with me on a date—which she did not know about! The evening of Uncle John's visit, I came home and in the excitement of company, I forgot about the strand of pearls around my neck. They were the first thing Mother noticed as I greeted our company and she did not hesitate to verbally "dress me down" in front of visitors for my worldliness. Uncle John spoke up in my defense: "Ann, they are just pearls."

Right then and there I determined not to be caught living by holiness rules. Yet, I became trapped by traditions. I learned them well from my mother, who learned them from my grandfather and the Pentecostal church. My sister rejected them all and until near her time of death, blamed Mother for being too hard on her and too unrelenting in the rules. In truth, Mother was harder on herself than with any one of us. In our family, God's grace was freely offered to the sinner, but often not within the family.

Mother's family roots explain the basis of some of her fears.

She was born on July 24, 1907, to parents who had come to America like so many turn-of-the-century immigrants, seeking the American dream of freedom and plenty. Her father, Andrew Marton, came from a stern, hardworking, and respected Czechoslovakian family. These qualities served him well in making his way in a strange country whose language he could not speak, but they became a source of irritation to his oldest daughter—my mother.

A photograph of Mother taken in her teenage years speaks volumes of her rebellious years. Her only comment when questioned about those years was to admit she had been caught up into the flapper life style during the roaring twenties. One of her brothers confirmed that she had been a rebellious girl, hating the restrictions of strict Lutheran parents who insisted she attend catechism classes. Mostly, she rebelled against her family's European ways of thinking and living. She wanted to be an American and live like her friends.

My grandparents came to the end of knowing what to do with their oldest daughter and thought they had found a way to keep her in line by sending her to live with an uncle in Cleveland, Ohio, to attend a Lutheran school. Of those years, Mother shared only one story with me. Her father regularly sent her money for school supplies, which became a source of temptation when her best friend bought a pair of skates. As Mother related the story to me when she was in her seventies, her eyes lit up, remembering the freedom of "flying through the streets of Cleveland" on skates. But when her father heard what she had done with the money, he cut her off by sending all monies to her uncle. She kept the skates, but determined never to share anything with her father—he had taken away the one joy she had and it hurt her deeply.

At the age of seventeen, Mother chose to attend a secretarial school with the help of her uncle and the disproval of her father. A job provided clothes and money to attend the roaring twenties dance halls with her friends. She thought she was in love with a young man she met and stayed engaged to him for two years, unable to commit herself to giving up her independence and becoming a housewife. Beside that, she knew he drank too much, and that was something her father never did.

When my father walked into the dance hall, he saw a pretty, blue-eyed, blond young woman flirting with the men—the picture of a liberated woman. She did not hesitate to accept his offer for the next dance, but she resisted when he boldly whispered in her ear that he planned to marry her.

The tall, handsome career Marine with deep American roots, appealed to a young woman wishing to shake off her foreign roots to fit in with the swinging flappers of her age. Her new pursuer had a suaveness not found in the men from her office or in the men from the factories who sought her out at the dances.

Four months later, Mother entered into a religious world that completely met her by surprise. She felt betrayed by her husband, shocked by a holiness group of people expecting her to conform to their way of life, and shaken by an emotional encounter with a God she had never understood. Trying to adjust to all of this—sometimes reluctantly, sometimes with resentment—she struggled to find ways to fit into a Pentecostal minister's life, but only by giving up her enthusiasm for life. There seemed to be a rule against everything she once enjoyed, and eventually it became difficult to find equally enjoyable substitutes without feeling guilty for a desire for the pleasures of the world.

The day Mother became a member of the Pentecostal church, she became known as Sister Wilkerson. I think for Mother, the "sister" became her Christian name. She would never allow people to call her Ann. Her friend, Fay, who worked with Mother in the Coffee House Ministries in Greenwich Village, told me in answer to my curiosity, about how Mother responded to her as a friend: "Your mother was a very private person, never sharing anything personal. She called me Fay, but she wanted me to call her Sister Wilkerson. I didn't mind. I saw your mother like a holy mother who raised two boys for a great ministry, and I respected her for her faithfulness to God. I called her the 'blessed mother.'"

For years, Mother thought she must earn God's love and approval by keeping rules and doing good works in the Church; it became a heavy burden. We all suffered the effects of her limited concept of God's grace. Years later, she learned to have fun when she realized she did not have to earn God's love. She had missed out on so many of the pleasures of earth that God had pronounced good. She tried to conquer her addiction to rules; she no longer gave us the stern look, but some things she could never bring herself to do—amusement parks, and makeup and jewelry remained off limits!

By watching the way God patiently taught Mother the difference between traditions and the true laws of God, I learned about God's grace and God's "humor." I had a good laugh when my brother told me Mother had not hesitated to go to the Coney Island amusement park with Teen Challenge workers to share the Gospel with hundreds of people. A few years later, with my young children in hand, she took them to the boardwalk in Asbury Park, New Jersey, and played games, dropping her dimes into the slot to win a prize for her grandchildren. We noticed her glee when she won a dishtowel—a prize she could keep. My children called her the "gambling grandmother." They find it difficult to believe we never had fun times with our mother.

Mother's freedom from believing she had to earn God's love by her works, began when she stepped into a very different kind of world. In 1961, at Washington Square in Greenwich Village, Mother encountered a generation the likes she had never known: they were the beatniks, hippies, drug addicts, alcoholics, transvestites, runaways, college drop-outs, and others who had dropped out of society. This was a generation who kept no rules, and this is where Mother found her second calling.

The Coffee House ministry started with one woman who had a burden for the Village where she grew up. For years she had worked with a small group doing the work of evangelism on the streets. When Fay Mianulli heard of David's street ministry she wondered if he would consider a mission in the Village. It took Fay almost a year of prayer and talking over her idea with interested friends before she had the courage to approach David. At last she mailed David a letter dated March 14, 1961. Fay gave me a copy of her letter. It reads in part:

*Greetings from Greenwich Village—the home of beatniks, artists, poets, drug addicts and the emotionally perverted—what a field for evangelism. Permit me to give you a briefing on my person…I am a Christian worker, the Lord gave me a burden for this place and from 1947 to 1952 we labored here under a minister…I believe the Lord would have me open a store front where I can concentrate on intensifying the work of evangelism. This is a wonderful field for street meetings. In view of all your present demands, this may be a bit premature and not in His will, but I certainly can use your young people for outdoor work in this area.*

David invited Fay to the Teen Challenge Center for a personal interview, but then wasn't able to make the appointment. It was Mother who listened to Fay's story. Fay was Italian, cooked the best spaghetti and meatballs, and she was enthusiastic about everything in life, especially about serving the Lord. Mother did not appreciate being pushed into anything and she had always been on her guard against people transparent with their emotions. Fay was not a pushy person, but she did express her emotions about all things good. When Mother began putting Fay off until David returned, Fay's enthusiasm could not be restrained; her concern for the Village outweighed Mother's reticence. So she had a suggestion: "Sister Wilkerson, why don't you come down to the Village and I'll give you a tour." Mother had heard about the Village, but had never ventured into an area without David or Don.

You can gage my mother's emotional response to the Village people who gathered in the Square by excerpts from my brother Don: "Mom used to go down to the Village on Sunday afternoons...on one of her visits she began answering questions put to her by a group of law students...before long a large group had gathered around Mom...as soon as the policemen saw a crowd forming, they came on the double. When they found that Mom was the cause of it all they told her that she couldn't go around doing things like this."

"I can't help it," Mom told the policemen. "I began by speaking to a few boys and all of a sudden all these others gather around to listen. I can't stop them from doing that."

On a number of occasions a policeman would tell Mom, "If you don't stop passing out that literature, we're going to have to run you in."

"Okay," Mom would say. "Get your paddy wagon ready." (*The Gutter and the Ghetto*, 143).

The crowds cheered her boldness and courage. Laughing with them, Mother quickly seized the opportunity to invite them to be at the Square the following Sunday to discuss the Gospel.

Mother never got "hauled in," but she did come back to Teen Challenge just as excited and emotional as Fay. Her face glowed with the pure joy of giving witness to the love and power of Christ to free people of their addictions. She told David stories of her encounters with the Village people with a great deal of enthusiasm. He recognized Mother had found her own ministry. It would be the ministry that gave her the greatest joy.

The combination of two prayer warriors and Spirit-filled "evangelists" were a team David could not easily ignore. He soon found himself walking the streets of Greenwich Village in search of a storefront for the first coffeehouse. He rented the former Den of Forty Thieves on MacDougal Street and renamed it the Catacomb Chapel. A few workers, a great deal of cleaning power, and a united prayer to God to bless the new venture, and they were opened for business. The Teen Challenge budget, already stretched buying only bare necessities, could not afford to authenticate the coffeehouse, so Fay and Mother dug into their own finances to serve coffee and a snack.

It was a coffeehouse unlike the others in the Village. The meager fare of crackers, coffee, and soft drinks was all they offered their patrons. But the Village regulars soon came to know the Catacomb Chapel as a place where they could sit in peace. They knew Mother and Fay, and the Teen Challenge staff wanted to engage them in conversation about the Bible and Christianity. People would crowd the entrance or sit on the step railings; some lined the sidewalks waiting their turn to have a religious conversation. The neighboring merchants complained that other people could not patronize their stores because of the crowds blocking their doorways. It didn't take long before the landlord notified the staff that there would be a considerable boost in the rent. For a while, Mother and Fay thought the coffeehouse days were over.

After praying for guidance, Fay led Don and Mother up and down the streets she knew so well in search of a storefront in the Village. Their search brought them to 190 Sullivan Street, and soon the Lost Coin opened for business. The advertisement read: "Come for a unique experience in religious conversation. Open Thursday, Friday, and Saturday evenings from 8-12 PM."

Fay had an exuberance about her that was irresistible. Everyone she met became her friend. Her heartwarming greeting to visitors made them feel at ease at the thought of sitting down for "a religious conversation." Of course, some entered boldly, ready to argue their own personal religious views. And some swaggered in with a switchblade in their belt. Neither Fay nor Mother had any fear of asking them to relinquish their weapons while in their territory. One frequent visitor remembered Mother boldly pushing a member of the Black Panthers firmly out the door when he became belligerent about being confronted with the Gospel.

Mother was a reserved person until she felt the Holy Spirit inspiring her to speak. Then she spoke with noticeable zeal and no one could doubt she believed every word she spoke, whether it was a biblical truth or a warning to the sinner to get serious with God. One of the men she warned to get serious calls her the "one who never gave up" in a tribute to her on his website. Mother would be shocked to see her name on the worldwide web! She would be sure to say to Mario that it was the Lord who never gave up on him. Mario's encounter with Mother was dramatized on the radio program Unshackled! and can still be heard on his website at www.misslink.org.

One of Mother's spiritual gifts was the discernment of the spirit within people she encountered. My brother Don tells stories of the way Mother exercised this gift in her years of encounters with people who resisted the Gospel. One story about a young beatnik especially stands out because the young man was Jewish and well trained in Old Testament history.

Stanley enjoyed talking with Mother, giving her every argument he could think of to resist the Gospel she shared with him. He kept coming back week after week, always ready for more "spiritual conversation" about portions of the Bible. Each week he made a point of telling Mother he was an agnostic.

After many months of pointing Stanley to the Scriptural proofs that Jesus was his Messiah, Mother told the workers they were not to engage Stanley in conversation any more. She felt that he had been told about the Gospel often enough and that there were others who were coming through the doors who had not been spoken to. Some of Mother's helpers may not have agreed with her approach, yet they respected her and were obedient to her orders. They continued to pray that the conversations with the young man would take root in his heart and that he might finally understand.

For the first few nights, Stanley just sat and listened, but he could not resist being involved in the conversations. Much to the workers' surprise, they heard him defending the Bible and Christianity. One night, Stanley came with a confession: "I finally understood what you were all talking about and I have given my heart to the Lord."

Similar stories of the truly lost within themselves, lost to society, to families, and lost to the truth about Christ's love and His power to free them from living in bondage to sin, will be told around the throne of God. Mother and Fay will be singing praises to the Lord for the mighty works He did in those six years in Greenwich Village.

In the Village, on the street, in buses and subways, by phone counseling or in letters, and at the Teen Challenge Center, Mother's calling to evangelism was affirmed over and over by the lives she touched because of her obedience to obey Christ's command to preach the Gospel and by her faith in the power of the Cross.

## CHAPTER 17

# THE TEEN CHALLENGE EXPLOSION

Teen Challenge's effect on the Church reads like a modern day continuation to the biblical Book of Acts. It contains the promise of the Holy Spirit to empower people to preach the Gospel to all nations beginning on the streets of New York City. It is the history of men and women who answered the call of Christ to give witness to the power of the Gospel. It is the story of many people who came to believe in Christ as their personal Savior. It is also the story of the expansion of the day of Pentecost within the twentieth and twenty-first centuries. It is, above all, the story of how God carried out His plan for ordinary people to establish His Kingdom on earth.

The Teen Challenge story is inseparably entwined with the Wilkerson story. It starts with the first family members who immigrated to America and reaches down into the fifth generation. In ways we cannot possibly know, the faith and works of each generation contributed to the foundation of the ministry of Teen Challenge. They were ordinary people who took seriously the teachings of Jesus—especially the one that taught us to "go into all the world and preach the Gospel to every nation."

We believe that God calls every believer to build His Kingdom on earth and the certainty of reaping a harvest is faith, obedience to God, and perseverance. Obedience to God was always a strong desire in the heart of my brother David, but he had also learned he could not preach with boldness without the power of the Holy Spirit.

The desire for a visitation of the Spirit became a cry within his soul—it was the call of the Holy Spirit to present himself a living sacrifice for Christ and His Kingdom. There could be no peace, no sweet fellowship with the Lord, and no rest until David responded to the Holy Spirit. David poured out the cry of his heart to God until the Spirit began to speak within him, revealing the very heart and mind of the Lord. By faith, David responded, not knowing what it all meant and where it would lead him. He committed himself to be obedient to Christ no matter the cost, and he trusted in the Holy Spirit to empower him to do the works of Christ.

The results of his initial act of obedience were published in the book, *The Cross and the Switchblade*, in 1963. Just as Luke, no doubt, had a burning desire to record the mighty acts of the Holy Spirit, so David wanted to publicly spread the news of what the Holy Spirit had begun to do in New York City among the gangs and drug addicts. He was introduced to two excellent Guidepost writers, John and Elizabeth Sherrill. Together they produced a bestseller that has been printed in many languages and is still in print today.

After reading the manuscript and assuring himself it was true to the events as they had happened, David admits he had reservations about the last chapter that talked about the Pentecostal aspect of the ministry. He had spent three years trying to get the social agencies in New York to accept Teen Challenge as a legitimate program for addicts and to gain the cooperation of the courts. David feared the chapter about the baptism of the Holy Spirit evidenced with speaking in unknown languages, would made them the "laughingstock" of these institutions. If they were to be labeled "Holy Rollers," David believed they would never be able to convince anyone of the successes of spiritual therapy with addicts.

It was the publisher, Bernard Geis, a Jewish man who challenged them "to get into the baptism of the Holy Spirit and write about it the way we feel." When I read this man's response to writing about the baptism of the Holy Spirit, I thought of the many times in history God caused His will and purposes to be accomplished by people who did not necessarily believe God was involved. David's book would stir many people in the Protestant and Catholic churches around the world to seek an outpouring of the Holy Spirit. People marveled at the story of a ministry to gangs and drug addicts, but it was the evidence of the power of the Holy Spirit still present in the Church that heightened people's curiosity to inquire about a present day visit of the Spirit upon believers.

After the publication of the book, David, Don and Mother, along with the staff at the Teen Challenge Center, were inundated with telephone calls from as far away as Europe. Letters poured into the office with requests to hear the story in their churches. A deluge of ministers and evangelism workers from many denominations continually arrived at their door for months. My brothers were astonished that the book had become a powerful influence in a new outpouring of the Holy Spirit in the traditional churches.

I recall Mother telling me of her amazement when she was introduced to one of the visitors—an Episcopal priest who had traveled all the way from Houston, Texas. Graham Pulkingham wanted to observe the Teen Challenge programs hoping to discover how to duplicate them in his city. At the end of his visit, David felt led of the Spirit to lay hands on the priest to be empowered for the mission God had given him. Pulkingham later testified to his congregation that the "very foundation of my soul shook violently," and he believed his prayers for a powerful ministry were being answered. Soon after his visit to Teen

Challenge, he led his church in the establishment of one of the first covenant communities modeled after the early Church's communal living.

Another visitor whom my brother Don especially enjoyed was David du Plessis, who became known as the first Pentecostal to establish spiritual unity with Protestant and Catholic charismatics. The Assemblies of God defrocked him in 1961 because of his "liberal views" but he was reinstated in 1980. When his travels brought him to New York, he gravitated to a place of welcome and spiritual renewal at the Teen Challenge Center. His stories about a worldwide spiritual awakening broadened my brothers' knowledge of a new outpouring of the Spirit. They were in awe that God had used the book in many nations as a testimony to the Pentecostal power still present in the Church.

The Teen Challenge story also caught the interest of the media. Television and radio talk show hosts were eager for David to tell their audiences the story of the religious revival on the streets of New York City. Life and Time magazines did a favorable spread about the successes of the program; all the city's newspapers featured the story with pictures and articles about the first known religious drug rehabilitation program in America. Suddenly David found himself being considered an expert on drug addition.

Once the publicity spread throughout the country, everything escalated beyond anything they could have imagined. The never-ending whirlwind of calls, visitors, letters, invitations to speak, put new demands on David and Don and the staff. Changes were inevitable—and they would call for great sacrifices for everyone involved with the ministry—especially for David and Don and their families. There was no time to ask: "Can we do this? Do we have the spiritual and physical strength to respond to so many people in so many places? How will our families survive?" Instead, the Holy Spirit carried them beyond their limitations and infused them with a power they had not yet experienced. By now, they had seen the mightiness of the Spirit and came to the conclusion He had only begun the "good work" He had started.

David had given no thought to the publication bringing worldwide acclaim to Teen Challenge or that life would never be the same at the Center—or for himself and his family. And he hadn't expected an outpouring of financial support for the ministry. People who read the book were moved to regularly support the ministry; many of them wanted help to establish a similar drug program in their own communities. David and Don were pulled in two directions: the needs of New York were great and the call for help around the world would become even greater. But they would not abandon the pressing needs of New York City.

As the Brooklyn ministry grew so did the need for space, staff, and finances. Early on, when it became vital to the spiritual growth of the men crowding in at the Center, a farm had been purchased in Rehrersburg, Pennsylvania. David wanted a safe and secluded, rehabilitation-training center for the men who had spent a few months in the Brooklyn Center. The need for a larger induction Center became and ongoing prayer request.

After a long, tedious and disappointing search for a place to build, they were brought back to the street where they had started. The purchases of two buildings and land on Clinton Avenue where Teen Challenge had begun served as apartments for the staff, a small apartment for Mother, and another for Don and Cindy. The third purchase would provide land for the construction of a new Center. A letter of appeal to the donors raised half the money needed for the new Center. A philanthropist, who had taken an interest in the drug program, gave a large grant that covered the rest of the cost. The new Teen Challenge Center was completed and dedicated to the work of the Lord in 1965.

Spectacular stories of outstanding events in history, or of people who left their mark on the world, are often turned into movies. David was staggered with the worldwide response to the book, so you can imagine his shock to receive inquires from Hollywood to produce a movie based on the book—a book about a Pentecostal religious event! Our family had avoided Hollywood, and anyone connected to this worldly enterprise, as we would a plague. Now the enemy of our souls pounded at David's door. Most naturally David took the matter before the Lord and prayed for a Christian to play the lead role and a producer who would understand the message of the story.

Pat Boone, a well-known Hollywood actor, showed a keen interest in producing a film based on the book about Teen Challenge. He expressed his desire to buy the movie rights and have David play his own part in the movie. David responded with a quick and firm "no" to Pat's acting suggestion explaining he had a calling to preach, not to acting. David reiterated his determination for a Christian other than himself to play his part.

It would take several years to discover a Christian producer who would buy the rights to the book and to find a suitable actor to play David's part. The rights were sold for the small sum of ten thousand dollars and divided between five people—David gleaned two thousand dollars for the ministry. When asked who would play David's part, Dick Ross, the producer replied, "A friend of yours, Pat Boone!" And Pat had a message for David: "I have experienced the last two chapters of the book."

The movie, produced in 1969, became an instant success. Day after day at the Center, they received reports of many people who had come to the Lord through watching the movie.

While David responded to hundreds of invitations to tell the story of Teen Challenge in churches and in auditoriums in America and later in Great Britain and Europe, Don assumed greater responsibility for the Brooklyn Center. David spent little time in his new office. More often Don sat at his desk while someone else occupied his small office. It became obvious and providential that Don should be officially appointed to take David's place as the Director at the center in Brooklyn. Don told me he seldom knew what David felt about his leadership until he overheard David say to a minister friend whom he had just given a tour of the new building: "Don does all the work and I get all the credit." At that stage of the ministry, this was a true statement. Although David believed Don to be the man chosen by God to continue the work in Brooklyn, he found it difficult to compliment his "little" brother whom he had helped to mentor and guide since Don had learned to walk.

The decision to officially turn over the leadership of Teen Challenge to Don in 1966, marked a turning in the nature of David's future ministry. He had come to a crossroad: he could go forward on a new road, or remain as the chief spokesperson on behalf of the Brooklyn Center ministries. It seemed the choice had been made long before David came to that crossroad; the Holy Spirit had already mapped out a ministry to reap a harvest in more fields than David could imagine.

David called his new evangelistic outreach The David Wilkerson Youth Crusades. His audiences looked much different than those on the streets of New York. They were made up of church teenagers he called the "goodniks"—middle class kids who were restless and bored with their lives. David was labeled an alarmist because he told parents and church leaders that their children were being seduced into a life of bondage to drugs, alcohol, and lawlessness. Few parents, ministers, or school officials believed these young people would be the next generation to be addicted to drugs.

For eight years, David traveled the country warning about the sins of society reaching deep into the Christian community. This ministry proved to be as heart-wrenching and exhausting for David, as had the Teen Challenge work. Years of traveling by airplane, and having to leave his family to help other families, plus raise sufficient finances to support his family and the staff needed to manage the crusades, took a huge toll on his body. He prayed for a way to lift the stress of traveling and broaden the scope of ministry to the Church.

In July of 1974, David and his family and the crusade staff moved to Dallas, Texas. David had decided to launch an entirely new ministry, calling it World Challenge. Texas would provide a slower pace of living and a place from which he could broaden his pulpit through the publication of his sermons, and a more centralized state would help cut down the traveling time to the crusades.

After David's departure from Teen Challenge, Don took full responsibility over all the programs and of raising money for the mounting daily needs. By then, he had been handling the establishments of workable programs, enlisting staff willing to work for pittance, teaching Bible classes, traveling to churches to talk about the ministry and to raise funds. Plus, he had been taking time to talk one-on-one with a constant stream of people with a myriad of problems.

Then after thirteen years of expanding the ministries in New York City, Don and his family were involved in yet another miracle. In 1974, the Brooklyn Teen Challenge purchased a year-round campground situated on Lake Champion, New York. The establishment of a thriving inner city ministry called Cure Corp set in motion the idea of a place outside the violent neighborhoods where children and teenagers could breathe fresh air and hear the Gospel of God's love. Hundreds of children arrived weekly for a once-in-a-lifetime experience during the summer months. During the winter, the camp served as a men's rehab center and also a marriage retreat for couples that had been on drugs.

Don volunteered his family to live year-round at the camp, hoping to attract additional staff. It took two years to establish a well-organized program and to find people willing to live in the middle of a forest. Don and Cindy and their children have a variety of memories of the eleven years of being isolated from city life. Julie, their youngest, made friends with a Canadian duck and was devastated when the bird eventually flew north. Todd was relieved to be in a car when he saw his first bear blocking the road to their house. Kristy remembers almost freezing to death in her determination to walk four miles home from school through a snowstorm. Cindy remembers black ants invading and occupying their closet doors and walls, and squirrels and bats scurrying down the chimney. Don remembers having to travel constantly to secure funds for the country Teen Challenge Center and juggling his time between the country and the city programs.

They all made sacrifices for the sake of the men, women, and children who needed the kind of help the ministry offered. The sacrifices that came with living in isolation were offset by the joys of ministry to children and adults whose stories of changed hearts and minds are now being passed on to their children and their grandchildren. In ways both great and small, Don and his family impacted each life by entering into the life and times at Lake Champion.

## Chapter 18

# THE WORLD CHALLENGE MINISTRY

Our father's death in 1960 had set in motion changes in the family that none of us could have envisioned. Now David's move to Texas would set in motion new changes within the family. Except for Nan, we would all eventually move to Texas—and we would wonder why seasoned northerners like us voluntarily gave up the majestic mountains of many colors and the beautiful glistening snow of the winter.

With David and his family, it became a matter of finding a centralized location that would decrease the amount of time in traveling to his crusades. After studying the map, Texas seemed centrally located so that he could travel by bus in about the same amount of time it would take to fly to each speaking engagement. You see, David had a fear of flying—a very agonizing fear that reached deep into the pit of his stomach and took up residence just before flights, during flights, and afterwards when he thought about the next flight.

Even though these "fear flights" were missions for the Lord, they did not lessen their impact upon David's health. He became alarmed when his body showed physical signs of a stomach ulcer. Memories of Dad's painful illness with stomach ulcers that eventually caused his death prompted David to find ways to cut down the stress of flying. He had promised himself that he would never subject his own family to the throes of an attack that he had witnessed as a child.

But that frightening event would be replayed in David's family. After a rough flight that terminated in an emergency landing, David arrived home weak and doubled over with pain declaring he'd never again get into an airplane and then emphasized his decision by promptly passing out.

After several days of blood transfusions and intravenous therapy, the doctor performed a successful surgery. David, like Dad, had a predisposition to stomach ulcers periodically aggravated by an overload of both good and bad stress. Flying became the worst of his fears and an ordeal he determined never to face again. So out came the map; he laid it on the hospital bed and prayed. When Gwen came to visit he made a surprising announcement: "We're moving to Texas, and from now on I'll travel by motorbus."

Traveling in the comfort of a customized bus energized David's thoughts about traveling to crusades. Now he looked forward to leaving the driving to someone else while he slept, studied and prayed, and used the traveling time as an occasion to write several books. It also afforded him time to dream of how he would settle into this next phase of his ministry, in a state he had adopted as home for his family and ministry.

The dream of a ranch and a school to train Teen Challenge graduates, situated in the lush green, rolling hills east of Dallas began to form in David's mind, as did words to break the news to his family of his new plans. Fully aware of how much Gwen loved her home in a safe neighborhood in Dallas and the easier pace of family life in a southern city, David chose a quiet night after dinner to paint the best possible description of his dream.

A few weeks later, David signed the papers to purchase a 360-acre ranch. What many people do not know about my brother, David, is that he enjoys developing land and laying out plans for buildings to house ministries—and he's pretty good at interior decorating, too. Ask Gwen and she will tell you about the sheer joy David had in laying out Twin Oaks, and how he chose the décor of their new home while she was busy with the wedding of their firstborn child, Debbie.

David began developing the ranch by securing mobile homes to house each family, until small, ranch style houses could be built. He invited my brother Jerry and his family, who had been traveling with The Cross and Switchblade film, to become a part of World Challenge. This meant adapting to the very slow pace of country Texas living. While Jerry helped clear the acreage and served as a relief Crusade bus driver, he also managed the sale of literature during the crusades. His wife Eve found her niche in the offices helping to respond to thousands of letters asking information about the ministry and requests for David's books and sermons. Eventually the Lindale post office had to enlarge their facilities to accommodate the mail put out and received by World Challenge and the other ministries who flocked to East Texas. God's country, as some called the area, became home to numerous Christian ministries.

I remember Mother's strong reaction to David's request that she move to Twin Oaks Ranch. Leaving the Teen Challenge ministry where she had thrived on witnessing in the Village, on subways, on buses, and on the streets seemed unthinkable to Mother—she was not a country dweller. Even though she would have two of her "boys" and their families nearby, she balked at leaving Teen Challenge after fifteen years of ministry. But David insisted because of her age. Mother almost had to be lassoed to move her to Texas!

She was not happy when the decision was made for her, even though we all knew she needed the protection of her family. In Texas, she felt isolated from the world she had come to love. "There's no sinners to witness to," she complained to me by telephone. Mother still worked in the office as she had done at

Teen Challenge, but she often spoke of being lonely. To ease the boredom of country living, every day she made a fifty-mile roundtrip to Tyler, a city of 75,000 people, to shop and eat at Luby's Cafeteria. Eating at Luby's became a tradition, one she handed down to me. And now I to my children and my grandchildren—it has become a place where we can bond as a family when no one wants to cook, and it is often the setting for telling family stories.

The Twin Oaks Training Center grew to accommodate Teen Challenge graduates from many cities. Some students trained to serve as directors of Teen Challenges throughout the United States. David and a staff of teachers gave them tools for evangelism: to know the Word, to live the Word, to become people of prayer, and be empowered by the Holy Spirit to preach the Word. At the same time, David continued his crusades and writing sermons and books for publication.

Eventually, David sold the ranch to YWAM Ministries and moved to a smaller piece of land nearby. A large metal building housed the offices and literature department. He had scaled down his ministry to national crusades and writing, but he still held yearly crusades in New York City, and walked the city streets praying for the spiritual needs of people lost to addictions. Then he took a long overdue sabbatical to rest his body, refresh his soul, to spend time with his family, and to write down thoughts that had been burning in his heart.

Over the years, David's preaching style never changed, but more and more the content took on a prophetic tone. David refused to call himself a modern day prophet; he referred to himself as a "watchman" praying over our nation and observing the events that were determining the future of America. In 1973, he recorded these thoughts in his book, The Vision, which was republished in 2003 to address the events of the new century. His first book about Teen Challenge gave David a public forum to warn our nation about the drug culture; The Vision gave him a pulpit to warn people of God's judgments upon our nation if we ignored the rule of God. Often he was referred to as a doomsday preacher, but David never saw himself as an "end times" prophet pronouncing inevitable doom. His concern focused on the backslidden conditions within the Church and a society that more and more ignored God. He was a crier to tell people to fear the Lord, repent and be saved.

David's life in Texas did not consist of constant crusades or writing sermons and books. There were times to relax and have fun. I remember visiting Mother during the Fourth of July and being told that David had prepared a fireworks display. It was the first Wilkerson fireworks I'd ever seen. Mother sat comfortably in a lawn chair enjoying the colorful works flashing in the sky, but more so seeing David act like a kid with his first firecrackers.

Those years, however, had their dark side. Gwen and their two daughters, Bonnie and Debbie, all had cancer. Gwen was diagnosed with breast cancer and the thought of disfigurement would add to her battle to regain her health and stamina. David stayed at her side, silently crying out to God on Gwen's behalf. In his private times of prayer, he could not contain the depth of his despair; the inward cries became audible groans before God. Gwen did regain her strength and emotional stamina, but that did not prepare her for the shock of learning that her oldest daughter had also been diagnosed with cancer.

It was four years after Gwen's mastectomy when they were told that Debbie had been diagnosed with colon cancer. The family wondered if she would survive the complications caused by the toxic drugs used in her chemotherapy. Debbie's recuperation was a slow process; it was Gwen's victories over fear that helped her to comfort Debbie and give her hope.

In 1991, the fright and agony of a diagnosis of cancer would be played out all over again when doctor's discovered Bonnie had endometrial cancer. The heartbreaking news was announced to David while Gwen was once again in the hospital waiting to have a second mastectomy. By much prayer and successful medical procedures, mother and daughters survived cancer. Gwen wrote a book about the victories she and her daughters have celebrated, appropriately titled *In His Strength*.

In times of great suffering when perplexities cause as much pain as our trials, we have an inward resource that immediately gives us hope. It is not necessarily a hope that we will be delivered from all adversity, but it is the knowledge that the Spirit of the living Christ is with us through our trials. We know this to be true, not only because we witnessed our parents' faith and prayer life, but also because we each have experienced His presence to be real.

In these struggles, such as those experienced by David and his family, and later in my own family, we have come to understand the importance of being baptized in the Holy Spirit. It is the Spirit who gives us comfort. More importantly, He helps us to pray during the darkest hours of our life. When our hearts are broken, when our spirits are weighted down with perplexing questions, we know the Holy Spirit will assist us—often giving us the gift of an unknown language to express the deepest thoughts and prayers that we cannot identify. Using this spiritual gift takes us to a new level of faith and always results in a greater understanding of our trials and strengthens our ability to endure with peace. In the Spirit-filled life, we are empowered to "jump over walls" that we could never surmount on our own strength.

In spite of horrendous trials, David's vision for the Kingdom of God has never diminished. He grieved, he cried out to God, he questioned the depth of his faith, but he never doubted God's love or God's greatness. He simply refused to be daunted by whatever darts of evil Satan aimed at him or his family or by trials common to all people. As had our father, David held the plans and purposes of God in his heart until they became his own.

He came through his trials with a new vision. In 1985, after a serious discussion of the spiritual needs of the world, David and

Don collaborated on enlarging the World Challenge missions program. David had already been supporting missionaries and evangelism projects in Haiti and South America. He hoped, with Don's help, to build a strong missions effort in Europe and Asia. Soon after this discussion, Don resigned as the director of the Brooklyn Teen Challenge after twenty-five years of ministry and moved to Texas to direct the World Challenge missions program.

Groundwork for a new missions effort had been laid years before through the publication of David's book, *The Cross and the Switchblade.* People involved in the European and Soviet Union underground church, had told extraordinary stories of how widely the book had spread. After the fall of the Russian empire, they discovered the book had been hand typed on letter-sized paper and passed from house to house until the pages were frayed from constant usage. In many countries, Christians reproduced the book in their own language.

People all around the world had heard the Teen Challenge story and had been inspired to seek an outpouring of the Spirit in their own nation. Many church workers and leaders longed to hear the story firsthand; invitations to speak in Europe and the former Soviet Union countries began pouring into the Teen Challenge and World Challenge offices. Both brothers felt the burden to respond to these "Macedonian calls" for help, but at the same time they were also hearing another call for help.

That call came from people in New York City who were well acquainted with the ministry of Teen Challenge. They had prayed that David would come back into the city to meet the spiritual needs of a new generation. The idea of going back to New York had been stirring in David's heart for a long time. As Gwen so succinctly describes her husband in those days of the seventies and eighties: "Living on the ranch had taken David out of New York City, but it had not taken his love for the city's people out of him."

David and Don agreed that there could be a way to

respond to all the pleas for help by establishing a strong missions-oriented congregation in the middle of New York City. It would take them in a new direction, but not into unfamiliar territory. They were confident that God would provide for the establishment of a church just as he had for the program for gangs and addicts.

CHAPTER 19

# REVIVAL ON BROADWAY

I have likened the story of Teen Challenge to a modern continuation of the biblical book, The Acts of the Apostles, which describes the ministry of the first church. I see my brothers as a twentieth (and now twenty-first) century Paul and Barnabas. As to their callings to the ministry to gangs and addicts, David received his in a spectacular way, as did Paul in his call to preach the Gospel, and like Paul, David is obedient to his calling. Barnabas, who played a significant role in establishing the Church, was suddenly thrust into a new ministry with Paul. My brother, Don, had a leadership role in establishing Teen Challenge, never expecting to find himself in a pastoral ministry with his brother.

David gave voice to the inner cry of God to use him to help meet the spiritual needs of New York City. Realizing the monumental task of birthing a new church, David chose to enlist two men whom he trusted and knew would faithfully share the burdens with him. Along with his brother and his friend, Bob Phillips, they were to be a team, each with their own ministries, that would cover all the spiritual needs of a congregation and be patterned after the New Testament church to reach out into the city and beyond.

In Don's latest book, he writes about the call he received from David to join with him once again in a New York City ministry—

this time to establish a church: "My thoughts ran a wide spectrum from excitement, to fear, to total reluctance, but the Holy Spirit spoke to my heart once again and issued a second call to the asphalt jungles of New York. But this time I saw the marriage of evangelism and discipleship under one roof through a local church. I was privileged to be one of the pastors" (Called to the Other Side, 122).

After over ten years of country-based ministries, David and Don and their families moved to the heart of the city that never sleeps. Living in Manhattan became a challenge, getting re-accustomed to sirens screaming, horns blowing, loud street cursing, taxis weaving in and out of traffic with frightening speed, the night almost as bright as the day, people pushing in the rush to and from work—and who can find an ordinary grocery store in the city when you need a loaf of bread? Only visitors like me seemed to notice the many stresses of living in a large city. David and Don fit right back into the hustle and bustle and excitement that comes from another call of the Spirit to the city they loved.

The first services of the new Times Square Church were held in October, 1987 at the Town Hall Theater at 43rd and Broadway, with a packed crowd. News spread fast that David Wilkerson had come back to New York. Many Christians, who had prayed for years to see a New Testament based church in mid-Manhattan attended the first services—they came to welcome David and Don and to give their support.

Quickly they outgrew the Hall and moved to the Nederland Theater at 41st Street and Broadway. Eventually the World Challenge Board of Directors and David decided there was a need for a permanent home and one with more seating capacity. In March of 1989, they purchased the Mark Hellinger Theater at 51st and Broadway. In large letters the marquee read: TIMES SQUARE CHURCH—REVIVAL ON BROADWAY. Everyone on Broadway knew a different kind of "play" had come to town— this one would have a long showing. Audiences would hear words and music never before played on a Broadway stage.

People flocked to the theater, coming from the five Boroughs, Long Island, New Jersey and Connecticut. A constant stream of visitors to the city somehow found their way to the new church on Broadway. During a communion service, David wanted the congregation to see the diversity of the church. He invited a person delivered from drug addiction, one from prostitution, a former homosexual, and an ex-convict to join him on the stage. And he asked one person from nations in Asia, Europe, South America, Africa, and North America to join the people reborn through the ministry of the church. The evidence of the ministry of the Holy Spirit in the church stood hand in hand, and together with the congregation they gave praise to the Lord in remembrance of His sacrificial death on their behalf.

At each service, people from many denominations entered into the worship along with the Pentecostals. People liked the anonymity that the large theater afforded them: Wall Street brokers sat with ex-convicts, CEOs sat with the unemployed and homeless. Entertainers from Broadway and off-Broadway shows came to investigate the new "show"—some of them Christians willing to offer their talents for the Kingdom of God.

The preaching and teaching of the Scripture held prominence in Times Square Church; their goal was to preach "the whole counsel of the Word." For years, the Pentecostal pastors were like general practitioners who responded to the entire spiritual needs of the congregation. Occasionally, an evangelist came with his expertise, usually to arouse the people to evangelize their community. Since the 1950s, "specialists" in the field of faith healing, positive confession, prosperity, intercessory prayer, evangelism, and the gifts of the Holy Spirit began movements that took on the look of denominations. Christians became followers of the specialists and often the Word of God narrowed down to one teaching on which people were spiritually fed. When televangelists entered people's homes, the scope of the

Body of Christ was broadened for many people, but the wholeness of the Body began to weaken for lack of fellowship with like believers, and from loss of opportunities for hands-on service to God, and especially for the lack of a complete knowledge of the Bible.

In the Manhattan church, the pastors set out to meet all the needs of the individual. They were diverse in ministry, each with his particular style of preaching, working together to meet the whole need of the person. At first, David was the "prophet-like" preacher that railed against the people's sins and the sins of the nation. Don took on the role of the shepherd to lead and guide the people into greener pastures. David had to learn to pour oil on the people's wounds; Don said he couldn't bring himself to prophesy in the presence of his brother—but occasionally he couldn't constrain prophetic words.

In David's World Challenge message "Unrelenting Love," he confesses to the narrowness of his early messages: "I preached messages on the evil conditions in the Church. I despaired over the deplorable state of so many of God's people. And I set out to correct these things with a sword and a sledgehammer. I struck at compromise and smashed everything in sight. And in the process, I brought people under condemnation that never should have been."

The joy of the services spoke of the satisfaction the congregation had with their pastors and their God. The fellowship among the people revealed their love for each other. The hush over the people when one of the men approached the pulpit to preach showed their reverence for the Word of God. The concerts of prayers, hours before the services began, spoke of their earnestness to see the power of the Holy Spirit change the hearts of all who entered the church doors. A full church at the weekly prayer meeting let the pastors know they were serious in winning people to Christ.

Not everyone who entered the theater knew about the

Pentecostal experience; a few had a distorted understanding of the gifts of the Spirit. David would not allow a message in tongues to be given publicly—he said it would be too confusing and distracting, and that the Word preached from the pulpit was sufficient. Some of the old-time Pentecostals disagreed and soon lost interest in a church where they were not allowed to display their "gifts."

Other people had to be taught how to worship. Joyful praise came easy. People liked to clap to the upbeat music that began each service. It made them feel good. I remember the feeling of excitement I felt on my first visit to the theater. Before the curtain parted, the congregation could hear the sounds of the orchestra rising higher and higher. In anticipation of the parting of the stage curtain revealing a robed choir, the congregation rose to its feet without anyone directing them to stand. The trumpets blared, the drums boomed throughout the theater, the organ and piano joined and the people clapped still unsure of the melody. Suddenly, recognizing the song, in one voice they sang out: "Make a joyful noise! Sing unto the Lord!" One could not sit stone-faced, unmoved by the orchestra and voices lifted heavenward.

Quiet times of waiting on God and listening for the "still, small voice" of the Holy Spirit to guide them into devotional worship to Christ were not so easily learned or understood. Often David would ask the people to be seated and wait quietly before the Lord and focus their minds on His majesty and greatness, or on His mercies and goodness. Those awesome times would end with a song of worship to the Lord, or a quiet concert of prayers of adoration when people lifted their hands to the Lord or wept, quietly voicing their love and gratitude to the Lord in their own way. The sense of the holy is an inspiring experience, one that became part of our spiritual life at an early age. David and Don taught the congregation to expect and revere the awesome presence of God in their midst.

Preaching the whole counsel of the word included teaching the congregation to meet the needs of people outside of the theater. Programs were put in place to feed the hungry, find shelter for the homeless, and take care of widows. Fay, who had given years of service working with Mother in the Coffee Houses of Greenwich Village, and now in the church, was provided a studio apartment in a building purchased for widows, unwed mothers and staff. She was thrilled to still be part of the Wilkerson ministries and proudly took me on a tour of the buildings introducing me to everyone we met—she knew them all by name and they all knew Sister Fay. There was great sadness for all of us who loved Fay when she went to be with the Lord in 2003. Fay is remembered as a woman of faith and an ardent witness of the Gospel. I remember, too, her ability to have fun and make others laugh.

In 1991, at the age of eighty-four, Mother returned to New York City to live near her two sons. She had served Teen Challenge for fifteen years, and had served in World Challenge as a counselor, responding by phone and letters to hundreds of people asking for spiritual counsel. In the theater, ushers reserved seats for "Mom Wilkerson" and her friend, Fay. The congregation regarded Mother as Fay did—a blessed mother. When I visited the church, I saw her sitting like a queen, while loving and kind people knelt beside her seat to express their love and appreciation for her sons' ministries. She would beam, often sharing some memory of her own past ministry at Teen Challenge.

Fay had always called her Sister Wilkerson—that hadn't changed over the years. But before she died, Fay told me about a milestone day when Mother did have a change in one of her rules. "Your mother and I stopped in a thrift store. She seemed attracted to the jewelry. I said, 'Sister Wilkerson, look at these beads, they match your blue dress. Why don't you buy them?' And guess what? She smiled and said, 'Okay.' I slipped them over her head. She wore them to church on Sunday."

I laughed with the delight of Mother's new freedom, remembering when she told me I looked like a Jezebel at the dedication of our first child. I had worn three strands of green beads that day!

I was with Mother the night she died in July 1997 in Lindale, Texas. It was difficult for me to watch her slowly slip into another world where we could not longer reach her. She did not have pain or the stress of dying, but I wanted to run from the bedroom. I had never experienced being with anyone in the dying process, and Mother lay frail, unable to take food or water, and I could not help her.

I cried out to God to help me through her death. Cindy, the caregiver who had faithfully attended Mother through the saddest stages of her illness, explained what to expect. We had Christian music playing softly. Suddenly, from the radio, I heard a burst of majestic music—it was the Hallelujah Chorus. Cindy whispered, "Ruth, the Lord is taking your mother home."

I believe the Holy Spirit arranged that sacred moment, giving beautiful earthly music to accompany the heavenly angels who had come to receive Mother's spirit to be with the Lord. I whispered to Cindy, "Let's sing 'Jesus Loves Me.'" Mother now knew Jesus truly loved her.

In 1995, after serving eight years as co-pastor with David, Don made a very difficult decision to resign from the Times Square Church.

When people ask me, "Whatever happened between your brothers, they seemed to work so well together?" I refer them to Luke who reported that Paul and Barnabas were filled with the Holy Spirit and spoke boldly in the Lord, but after a difference of opinion "…there followed a sharp disagreement between them, so that they separated from each other" (Acts 15:39 Amplified).

Don had successfully coped with hundreds of relational encounters with men in the Teen Challenge programs and with a large staff, but he had never found a way to cope with his brother's dogmatic nature. He came to believe that there would be no agreeable resolution to their present differences. For weeks, Don agonized over his decision to leave the pastoral ministry he loved, but he had no hope for resolving the turmoil of his spirit—leaving seemed his only choice.

It was sad for the congregation and the parting did not happen gracefully since neither of the brothers handled their differences well. David had years of making spontaneous decisions in his ministry without having to consult anyone; he made a strong effort toward teamwork, but long-standing habits aren't easily erased. Don believed he was no longer valued as a co-pastor since he was no longer consulted in important leadership decisions.

David preached the Gospel with strong convictions, never wavering from the Scriptures and many hearts were convicted of sin and believed in Christ as their Savior. But when he was dogmatic in relationships, it tended to tear friendships apart. Don had learned how to appeal to Teen Challenge ministry workers to see both sides of disagreements; but with David he regrettably expressed anger that didn't abate with the sun going down. Separating gave each of them time to assess their own actions and find ways of being at peace with God and each other.

When David welcomed Don back to Times Square church to speak of his new ministry with Global Teen Challenge the congregation knew the brothers were reconciled. Don told the people about the spread of drugs that was destroying a new generation of addicts in every country and of his travels to train leaders for Teen Challenge centers. They recognized Don had truly been called "to the other side."

David and Don have always respected the diversity of each other's ministries and in the preaching of the Gospel they have remained unified—that bond remains strong. They have kept to their vision to respond to the calls for help in every nation. They have also come to understand that God had used their separation to accomplish greater ministries.

# CHAPTER 20

# CALLED TO THE OTHER SIDE

Don speaks frankly of the days after leaving Times Square Church not knowing what his next ministry would be, or even where his family would live.

"There were real fears on my part as to how my wife and I would survive. I began thinking of other jobs I might do in the secular field. Maybe I could drive a limousine or enter some kind of service industry position. For the first time in my life, I perused the want ads in the newspaper. One night I woke up in terror telling Cindy, 'We're going to lose our house. I don't see any way I can continue to make the mortgage payments.' The feeling of loneliness and gloom settled over me (or should I say that I allowed to settle over me) like a dark cloud. There seemed no way out of the fog." (*Called to the Other Side*, 135).

Unknown to Don, hidden in the fog was God's plan for an enlarged ministry. He was asked to be the Director of Teen Challenge International—the opportunity had come to him once before, but it was not the road he had wanted to take at the time. The offer to be a pastor appeared much more inviting—it had been a long-standing dream. Now, once again facing an uncharted path left Don feeling alone and helpless.

It seemed as if he was being taken back in time to begin a new

Teen Challenge work all over again—having to raise funds, train staff, and do more traveling than he had ever had to do before. He wondered if he had the strength to establish a global Teen Challenge—or even had the heart for it. Don took his perplexing thoughts and feelings to the Lord asking for guidance and strength to face a ministry that would probably be more formidable than the first.

A call from the missions' leader of the Assemblies of God in Central Asia presented a challenge Don could not ignore, but one he could not financially afford to accept. He had been invited to witness firsthand, the need for Teen Challenge centers in India. As Don always does, he presented the invitation and the need for money before the Lord. He heard the inner voice of the Spirit encouraging him to step out in faith and made plans to go to India. The Spirit's guidance confirmed to Don that he was about to embark on the ministry God had chosen him to do.

He was accompanied by his close friend, Jesse Owens, who would become a co-worker in the growing ministry of establishing Teen Challenges in many nations. A small grant of money paid for their expenses.

As Don walked the crowded streets of India and saw firsthand the immensity of the drug problems, the Holy Spirit once more sparked his zeal for the ministry. Once he fully accepted the calling and burden of God, the fear over finances was no longer a dark cloud hanging over Don. He had been delivered and healed of doubts and unrealistic expectations.

Don realized his need to be constantly energized and guided by the Holy Spirit. Finances, trained workers, buildings, and supporters for Global Teen Challenges became a huge task. The workers were facing needs far worse than Don had known in America. There were few spiritual churches from which to draw leadership or finances. Drug addiction, prostitution, violence, and poverty had overtaken nations whose governments and churches had no solutions. Many government leaders welcomed help and did not frown upon the spiritual goals of a religious organization.

In a 2004 Global Teen Challenge letter to staff and supporters, Don gives the answer to why this ministry must forge ahead in faith: "When we look into the eyes of someone with a life controlling, destructive problem, we must be able to give that person a reason to live another day…to hope for a better life. It we can't give hope to the alcoholic, we have no business being in a ministry of recovery. If we can't give hope to the heroin or cocaine addict, we have no right to ask them to make a commitment that would bring change. One of the first things TC offers to the drug addict, prostitute, 'gang-banger' and other disturbed lives is that there is hope for change. And, we unashamedly let them know that this hope can be found in Jesus Christ."

Don has traveled to over eighty countries, and logged a million flying miles to share the miracles of Teen Challenge, and to train leaders to take up the call to preach the Gospel to a generation in bondage to addictions.

What keeps Don passionate about the spiritual needs of the world? I believe that it is the knowledge of God's compassion for a hurting humanity, and the strong conviction that God has called every believer to work in His kingdom. The choice to keep up the arduous work of flying around the world to establish an international ministry to a new generation of addicts is a determination to fall in behind generations before him who answered the call of God to "go preach the Gospel to every nation." His face has never turned in another direction. The passion of the Holy Spirit to bring people to the saving knowledge of Christ never ceases to resonate deep in Don's heart.

What has kept Don steadfast in his call? It is obvious to everyone who meets Don that it is, first and foremost, Don's love for God and the surety of God's love for him. It is also the faithfulness of past generations that has planted in Don the resolve to follow in their footsteps and trust God for the harvest. His zeal has certainly matched that of his grandfather and his father, but the scope of his ministry has far exceeded theirs, taking him into all the world to preach the Gospel.

And it is Don's trust in God, not in himself or a philosophical system, that has kept Don passionate year after year, in the midst of perplexing times, surrounded with the darkness of human tragedy, and in spite of the physical toll on his body.

Recently I asked Don if he planned to retire. He smiled and said, "Well, I might slow down a little. Of course, I do have a week of leadership training seminar in Russia, and so far in 2005, I have invitations for China, the Philippines, and Latin America." I somehow don't think Don intends to retire at sixty-five—if at all!

After Don left Times Square Church, David became senior pastor. His ministry has always reached into many nations through his books and printed sermons, but for years he restricted traveling in order to establish the ministries of the Manhattan church. Eventually, the call of the Holy Spirit to preach beyond the theater walls, took David down new roads where he encountered ministers much like himself, who had been hungering for words of encouragement, and a "fresh touch" of the Spirit.

At pastors' conferences, he challenges ministers and their wives, and church leaders to develop a greater intimacy with God, and to pray and fast until they are renewed in their spirit with a greater love and devotion to Christ. As David spoke of his yearnings for God and of his times of fasting and praying, he discovered that his own spirit was being renewed, and his heart was being baptized with a deeper devotion to the Lord, and for the people who sought out his ministry for a "word from the Lord."

One of the visiting ministers to the Times Square Church is David and Gwen's son, Gary. He is not a carbon copy of his father; he has had his own touch of the Spirit upon him to preach, but he has the same sense of being called as his father, his grandfather, and his great grandfather. Gary has taken up the call and the passion to preach the Gospel of Christ—and like his father, he speaks a clear message of the cost of being a disciple of Christ to the youth of America and in every country where he and David hold crusades.

Surprisingly, David took to the skies with his son to take pastors' conferences and youth crusades to Great Britain, Europe, Asia, and South America. In Europe, they found widespread despair and spiritual dryness. Ministers, who have struggled so long with spiritual apathy thought of giving up the call to preach. Both David and Gary projected new vitality with a message of hope and power; their message, calling church leaders back to their first love, stirred the audiences to pour out their hearts to the Lord. Revival broke out in the services. One man spoke of the presence of the Lord being so powerful that the pastors were broken and weeping as the Holy Spirit brought healing and restoration to lives and to marriages.

In a public letter to people who support the conferences, David shared his methods of conducting the teaching sessions:

*We have no workshops or classes on how to grow and expand your church. The program is very simple. We have four preaching services each day, with times of worship and ministry to both men and women, as we also focus on encouraging ministers' spouses. Our prayer is that all who attend will be challenged to renew their prayer life. The Holy Spirit digs very deep into hearts, and we have seen thousands come alive with new faith and a powerful touch of the Holy Spirit. Ministers of many denominations are weeping together, with deep repentance and incredible love for Jesus and for one another.*

What has kept David steadfast in his call? The call to past family generations and their obedience to God cannot be underestimated; they left us an immeasurable spiritual legacy to follow. Yet, beyond the call to a family, David has experienced a personal encounter with God not unlike the encounters of ancient men we learned about in our youth, who feared God and recognized that they had holy transactions with a God calling them out of the world to serve in His Kingdom.

David still holds visions in his heart of what he wants to accomplish for the Kingdom, and he keeps going forward toward these goals. He has always expressed shock and perplexity over Christians who think aging or a list of accomplishments exempts them from service for God. He does not picture himself and Gwen sitting on a front porch rocker surrounded by their grandchildren with no more cities to conquer. He sees himself following a great host of men and women, who marched triumphantly toward the "prize set before them," who harbored no thoughts of turning from their call, or from the command of Christ to preach the Gospel to all nations.

My father would have been amazed and very proud to see his sons doing greater works than either he or his father had done—or could have imagined. I believe Dad would be humbled by the realization that God had chosen the Wilkerson family to preach the Gospel of Christ to all nations. He would talk about his sons with great pride, but foremost in his heart, would be the joy in knowing that each of his children had believed in Christ as their Savior.

## CHAPTER 21

# THE LOST SON

I don't have all the answers to why the second son got lost in the family, or why he strayed far from God, or walked away from his wife and children, but I can tell you that there was a Shepherd searching for Jerry until He found him.

Beginning in the Barnesboro attic bedroom, a hierarchy was established between the two brothers: David was the leader and Jerry, the follower. The boys spent many hours playing board games in their attic bedroom, vying for the most points on the basketball court, and working together after school at a grocery store. In all these areas, they were almost equals, but not quite— David assumed the status of the older, more mature brother who handed down his clothes, taught his brother the ins and outs of the grocery business, and tried to keep Jerry on the straight and narrow path. But on the basketball court, Jerry had the upper hand.

Jerry loved sports and while David dreamed of preaching, Jerry dreamed of playing sports—especially basketball. Worldly dreams were not voiced in our household. If they had been, they absolutely would not have been given any credence. In those years, our parents could not entertain ideas beyond the holiness traditions, so Jerry kept his dreams to himself. He knew David would only laugh and give him a sermon on giving his life to preach the Gospel.

During their teen years, Jerry watched his brother drift further away from their childhood pleasures and times together, he felt alone and without direction. He knew he had not heard the call to preach as had his grandfather, and his father, and now David. More and more he lost the sense of being a part of the family; the camaraderie of the attic days were gone. The times of playing sports together became less and less. David seemed to treat him as if he was not quite capable of handling the grocery job, and it was evident that Dad focused his attention on the son who could sit and discuss the "things of the Lord" with his father.

Both boys enjoyed the privilege of going to Living Waters Camp to prepare the tents and fill the bed ticks with straw. Besides being fun, they liked the pleasure of feeling important to be working with men from nearby churches. At the camp services, David responded to the call to go forward to the altar to dedicate his life to the Lord. David speaks of camp days when he heard the call of God to preach the Gospel. Jerry never gave testimony to a call, but like all of us, he could not help being affected deep within his soul—the sermons were pleas to believe in Christ as the Savior of the world and warnings of the coming of the Lord.

In the boys' teenage years, Jerry seemed to drift more and more toward sports. I've often wondered, had Mother and Dad been free of the holiness traditions and considered the differences in their children as normal and had nurtured the hopes and dreams of each child, would there still have been one rebellious child, and one lost child in our family? I do not know the answer to my question. I suspect they may not have taken some of the dangerous paths had we been a closer-knit family.

David remembers an event when his actions caused a painful chasm between them, which evidently continued to cause David feelings of remorse. It is not a hair-raising story of a fight between two brothers, but one of a public humiliation of the younger brother by the older brother two years his senior.

One day a customer gave Jerry fifty dollars toward payment of a bill and Jerry lost the money. When David found out about it he called him a "ne'er-do-well" in front of a store full of people. Jerry took his apron off and walked out of the store. Realizing he had embarrassed his brother, David ran after Jerry, but he refused to turn around and give David a chance to make amends. From then on, David felt Jerry determined to shut him out of his life.

Recalling the story, I am reminded of Jerry's first music lesson when he walked out and never returned. A pattern had no doubt taken root and no one noticed; probably Jerry was unconscious of his inclination to walk away from problems instead of putting effort into solving them.

We seldom discussed our personal problems with our parents. From our father's sermons and in Sunday school classes, we did learn how Jesus handled people and situations, but I don't recall His teachings being personalized. I wish we had heard our parents say: "Jerry, there are better choices than walking away from your hurts and troubles." "Ruth, you are never alone; God is always with you." "David, charity begins at home. Go to your brother again; he needs to know you are sorry." "Nan, help us find a way to compromise so that you don't rebel against the rules."

David admits to a habit we all fell into. After Dad died, we did not keep in touch with each other. We were scattered between four states, and none of us could afford to visit the other. Plus, we were all too occupied with our own interests. However, I believe we lacked a close bond with our siblings because of the nature of our household—too many ordinary pleasures were taboo; there were few family fun times. I don't recall either Mother or Dad sitting down with us for a game of checkers. And card games were definitely forbidden! We ate together, listened while our parents prayed at family altar time, sat separately in the church services, and attended camp without ever meeting up with each other. This emotional disconnect, although unintended, left a void in us, and eventually affected each one of us deeply.

When Jerry or any one of us found ourselves with people who wanted our friendship, even in simple ways of playing games or conversations, we all struggled to establish close friendships. When Jerry met Eve, his wife-to-be, he met a large family that had bonded tightly together around a table where games and competition became a staple of life. Jerry liked their friendliness, but he could not bring himself to enter into their fun.

I recall, with shame, visiting my husband's family and taking along a book because I did not know how to converse with people who could not talk about "the things of the Lord." My husband had to point out that my actions showed a lack of love for others before I would put the book away. It became a challenge to change my ways. My brother, Don, speaks of having had difficulty socializing with people outside our church community. It became a hurdle we all had to find the courage to overcome.

Jerry and Eve met in the church and I played matchmaker for two shy people who were very much attracted to each other. After their marriage, they settled in the Pittsburgh area and began to raise a family. Jerry had a good job as a produce manager in one of the area's large grocery chains. His young family barely had time to establish a home, when Jerry was drafted into the army. Those were not good family days; Jerry learned a way to fit in with a worldly society by drinking with the crowd. As with Dad during his Marine days, Jerry had found a way to ease his fear of social encounters.

When they returned to Pittsburgh, what little family bonding we did have began to dissolve. When Dad died, the cords were so frayed that only Mother kept in touch with Jerry and their family. David admits that he was so busy winning souls that he neglected to keep in touch with his own brother. The truth is, we all neglected each other and weren't aware of the devastating effect of broken family relationships. In fact, we did not see our family as broken.

Then one day, we were all brought to our knees: Jerry was lost. Mother had just come back from visiting Jerry and Eve. She made an urgent plea to David and Don, and to me to pray for Jerry because he was drinking—and she did not mean social drinking. Mother feared Jerry might become an alcoholic.

It was Mother who took up the call to intercessory prayer. We each "said" our prayers for Jerry and went on with our busy lives. Jerry's drinking problem worsened—he missed work, sat hours drinking at a bar with his drinking buddies, and finally in disgust of himself and shame of revealing his condition to his wife and children, Jerry walked away from his marriage and his children. Jerry admitted to Mother: "When I'm out drinking...I just can't think of my family. Alcohol consumes my time, my thinking, my entire existence."

The night Mother called David to tell him Jerry wanted to kill himself, David came to realize his passive attitude toward Jerry. David cried out to God to save Jerry's soul, but he met the silence of God. And then it hit home in his heart; he had not written or spoken to Jerry for a very long time. A terrible conviction hung over David like a dark cloud—he had not cared about Jerry as a brother should. He remembered the Scriptures taught that to not provide for one's own family, was not only denying the Gospel, but were the actions of an infidel!

In our private times of praying, we united in constant prayer that Jerry would come to New York and find help within the family. Soon David received a call from Jerry. He was at the Port Authority building in Manhattan asking how to get to David's house. Jerry spoke his mind to David telling him that the store where he worked sold his book and his co-workers wondered if he belonged to that Wilkerson family. "Their question really made me feel lousy." David felt crushed when Jerry confessed that he knew his brother was out saving the world, but didn't care if he lived or died.

David obeyed the Scriptures, flew back to Pittsburgh with

Jerry, provided money to pay off debts, and found him a decent place to live. Then he helped secure the job he had walked away from. He introduced him to a pastor and urged Jerry to begin attending church. Before he left, David told Jerry he had two choices: "You can either go on from here, or you can go back to a bar and get smashed."

The pastor reported that Jerry chose to go back to the bar. We knew there was nothing the family could do but "pray through." This meant a constant prayer vigil over Jerry until he came to the decision he wanted to be clean and free. Today we refer to such a vigil as intercessory prayer. It calls for the sacrifice of time and energy and is the most powerful prayers one can pray. It is a cry to God that vibrates throughout the heavens. It is the kind of prayer talked about by James of the Bible who said: "...the earnest, heartfelt, continued prayers of a righteous man makes tremendous power available—dynamic in its working" (James 5:16b Amplified).

One day, Jerry showed up at the Teen Challenge Center claiming he was now ready for help, but at the end of two weeks he took off. Mother told Jerry they had done everything they could to help him and now they planned to turn him over to the Lord. This did not mean we would stop praying, but we would stop trying to rescue a man who was not ready to give up his life to the Lord—even if he was their own flesh and blood. Jerry needed more than human hands to reach out and try to save him; his destructive habits had become too deeply rooted in his soul.

My own family had moved to Queens, New York during this time. One day, I was shocked to open my door and find Jerry asking me for a place to stay. At first, I believed his argument that Mother and David did not understand him. I, too, had to tell him he needed help I could not provide. I grieved for Jerry—I felt helpless because I had my own spiritual struggles. I could not understand why God would allow both of us to be so lost.

I prayed, "Lord, how can I help my brother when I don't

know how to help myself? What has gone wrong with us? Is there any hope for us? What had happened to my castle of dreams? What had happened to the sweet love Jerry and Eve seemed to have for each other?"

Jerry continued to drink, holding on to a job in the city, but made no effort to see the family or his wife and children. In every crusade, David asked people to pray for Jerry. This time none of us gave up the prayer vigil. We were no longer fighting against Jerry's drinking or whatever sins had overtaken him—we were fighting against the powers of evil.

Don later recorded the results of those prayers:

*During the filming of the motion picture, The Cross and Switchblade, I went on location...and asked Pat Boone, who played my brother David in the film, if he would come and speak and sing at a youth rally in Glad Tidings Tabernacle...he said he would. There were only a few days before the rally and little time to advertise it.*

*The best I could do was to run a one-inch advertisement in the Daily News at the cost of eighty-five dollars. (Later I was to find out that I should not have advertised Pat's appearance. He was under contract which required that notices of all appearances had to be channeled through his agent.)*

*On the night of the rally, Pat, Shirley, David, and I met in the basement of the church and were preparing to go on the platform when David's crusade director...came to join us and said, "Your brother Jerry is in the service. He's sitting in the last row."*

*In very few words, David related the story of Jerry's alcoholism and spiritual condition to Pat and Shirley...I recall that most of the time Shirley Boone had her head bowed. After she and Pat sang and he shared a testimony, I introduced my brother who was to deliver the message of the evening. Just before he got up, Shirley put her hand on David's and said, "I believe this is Jerry's night." (Bring Your Loved Ones to Christ, 99).*

In a very different way, I also knew that it was Jerry's night for freedom.

It had started early that same Saturday when I was doing the usual end-of-the-week house cleaning. One of the women from our church called to ask if I would like to hear Pat Boone who was at a rally with my brothers in Glad Tiding Tabernacle in Manhattan. My immediate response was a definite "no." I had work to do, I dreaded taking the Long Island train into the city, and nothing out of Hollywood had risen to my level of interest. I did recall sitting in a Scranton diner when a friend stuck a dime in the jukebox and asked me what song I'd like to hear. I flipped through the titles and said: "April Love—I think I'll meet the man I will marry in April." I remember Pat Boone had sung the song that turned out to be prophetic. Even so, I was sure that wasn't a song he'd be singing at the rally.

I resumed dusting and vacuuming and wondered why I hadn't jumped at the chance of getting out of the house and the chores. Then I heard the "still, small voice" of the Holy Spirit, calling me by name: "Ruth, you need to go tonight. Don't worry about your work. Call Rosalie back and tell her you will go."

And that is how it happened that I found myself sitting in the first row, on the left side of the balcony, scanning over the congregation and still praying: "Lord, why am I here? I feel so rushed and tired. You must have me here for a reason." Some minutes passed before I saw Jerry sitting in the last row, on the right side of the sanctuary. I felt a surge of emotion going through my body, so powerful it left me trembling and weeping. "Ah, Lord," I whispered. "Now I know why you brought me here." I, too, knew it was Jerry's night to be set free!

I watched Jerry, wondering if he would bolt out as the service progressed from congregational singing to the Boone's duet. Then Pat gave a personal testimony to his salvation, and Don introduced David as the speaker of the youth rally. Jerry had not moved. David stepped to the pulpit, opened his Bible, but this time he electrified the congregation by announcing he was about to do something he had never done before. "Tonight," he said, "I am going to give an invitation to a single person." My heart raced, "Oh, no!" I thought. "He's talking about Jerry and Jerry won't like this."

David pointed toward the last row and spoke directly to Jerry: "Jerry, the last time we met I said you'd come back in your own way, when you were ready. Remember? Well, tonight you have come back. Jerry, I'm calling you in the name of the Lord. Make your decision to be on His side."

Seconds passed. People turned to look to see to whom David had spoken. Jerry paid no attention to the people around him. He ran to the altar and fell to his knees, shouting out his confession to God that he was a sinner. Pat Boone knelt beside Jerry and through Jerry's sobs asked him to repeat the sinner's prayer. Weeping could be heard throughout the congregation. My tears flowed so heavily that I could barely see what was taking place at the altar. I knew angels crowded the sanctuary rejoicing with us—a lost sheep had been found.

Later Jerry was asked how he happened to attend the youth rally. He told us of sitting at a bar leafing through the Daily News where he came across the small, illegal advertisement of Boone's appearance. Jerry liked Pat Boone's music and wanted to hear him in person—so he came, sitting in the last row, hoping no one would notice.

Broadway can never produce a dramatic play as the Holy Spirit had that night in the Glad Tidings sanctuary. He directed events and people, and each scene to the glory of the Lord—there were no mishaps. Without our knowing it, the Holy Spirit caused each of us to play our part flawlessly—it was God's play, not ours. In our hearts we joined with the angels in a standing ovation to the Lord.

Six months later, after a rehabilitation program at the Teen Challenge Training Center in Rehersburg, Pennsylvania, Jerry reunited with his wife and children. The TC director in Cleveland, Ohio, asked Jerry to represent their TC Center to churches in the middle states. Jerry showed the film, The Cross and the Switchblade, and gave a personal testimony to the power of Christ to set people free of addictions.

When David moved into East Texas to establish a training center for Teen Challenge graduates, he invited Jerry and his family to live on the ranch and become an active part of the World Challenge ministries. Jerry traveled with David to the crusades managing the distribution of literature and books published by David. Eve became part of the office staff helping to respond to hundreds of requests for David's writings.

Jerry and Eve have remained faithful to the Lord, to their family, and to the World Challenge ministries. They have had their share of trials and tribulations, but they have never lost sight of God's grace and goodness. They both hold to the faith of their parents and pass on that faith to their children and their grandchildren.

CHAPTER 22

# THE REBELLIOUS DAUGHTER

Many parents can tell stories of children leaving home to live a prodigal life. My family can tell that story, too. I wish I could say that our rebellious child eventually came back to the "faith of her fathers" and the comfort of family as in the story of the Prodigal Son in the Bible, and that her sister welcomed her with open arms—but that is not the way it happened.

This story is about my sister who rebelled against the restrictions of our religion and our home, blaming our parents and our church for her estrangement from God and family. It is also the story of my reaction to a sister I barely knew, and what I did know, I often did not like. It is a version of the prodigal child not told in the Bible, but lived out over and over in families. It is just as sad—maybe more so since there is so much waste of what God meant to be precious and comforting in family relationships.

It seemed to me that my sister did not like much of anything about our family or the church. Not her name, which she later changed from Juanita to Joan, not our Pentecostal worship or beliefs, not the modest clothing our parents required her to wear, and certainly not the strictness of the family rules. Our family life, taken all together, became a prison to Nan. In school with her peers, at the downtown dairy-bar and dance hall, from magazines and books, she had a glimpse of another world outside our little world and she longed to take flight, and sometimes did while in the boundaries set by our parents, much to their consternation.

She acted like a wild horse, straining at the bit—she balked and kicked against every teaching and every rule. Neither private lectures from our parents, or stern sermons of our father, or the discipline of spankings diminished her desire for the "things of the world." There were times when her heart seemed to soften by listening to camp teachers she admired, and by breathtaking stories of heroism told to us by missionaries from many countries. Yet she never made a total dedication of her heart to Christ. In her imagination, she thought it would mean losing out on the excitement of experiencing what society had to offer. She believed the battle in her mind could only be resolved by leaving home to go into the world to find a life more satisfying.

I have few memories of having a sisterly relationship with Nan. One I never forgot involved Mom and Dad listening to the presidential returns late into the night. They ended with the national anthem. She could hear the music in her bedroom where I had to spend the night because of giving up my room to company. Nan shook my shoulders to wake me out of a deep sleep and ordered me to stand up for the Star Spangled Banner. She knew as a first-grader, I believed the law required me to stand in honor of the national song. I stood swaying back and forth to keep my balance on the soft bed—which brought me fully awake to see Nan flat on the bed, laughing at my expense. I took revenge the next day by scaring her with a wild leap and a loud "boo" when she stepped onto the front porch.

Years later, when I told her this story we both had a good laugh, but then I asked her: "Nan, why didn't you pay attention to me? I often felt alone and unwanted." Caught between two older brothers and one younger brother who lived in their own attic world, I could have used an older sister to take me under her wings. Nan seemed shocked to learn I had felt friendless and alone. She had thought of herself as the only "sufferer" in the family.

My small world was far different than Nan's—I had no inward battle raging. Where she rebelled, I flourished; what she rejected, I accepted with great interest. Her heroes were from Hollywood; mine were the ancient people of the Bible. I could not understand why she wanted to offend God or our parents.

The saddest part of this story is that my parents and the Church taught us about the Great Commission to go into all the world and preach the Gospel of Christ, but often the mission did not include the lost children within the church family.

When Nan left home after graduating from high school, everyone seemed relieved, especially since she had been invited by Granddad Wilkerson and Maxine to live with their family in Mansfield, Ohio. Upon hearing of her rebellion against family and things religious, they hoped they could have a positive affect upon Nan. It did lead to Nan making a decision to attend an Assemblies of God Bible college, and Dad and Mother heard some promising reports of her interest in a missionary career. But lack of money kept her from returning for a second year, so out into the world she headed to support herself.

Nan moved to Washington, D.C., and easily found a clerking job and an apartment to share with three other girls. I was elated when she invited me to spend a week's vacation with the sister of one of her roommates. I remember Nan doing all she could to make it a fun time. She and her boy friend, Bob, who no one in the family had met, took me to an expensive restaurant where we sat across from General Eisenhower.

I believe Nan may have invited me to meet the man she intended to marry. I liked him, but once Mother and Dad heard he was Catholic, they felt Nan's choice was a way to show her anger toward them. Although they viewed her marriage as an act of rebellion, they accepted Bob into the family. We hoped Nan would establish a family of her own, but we were sure it would look nothing like the family in which she was raised.

Throughout Nan's marriage, her husband faithfully attended the Catholic Church, but Nan could not settle on any particular church. During those years we seldom saw Nan; when she did visit, we would hear all over again the same arguments of why she had rejected everything she had been taught: "I had to wear long stockings to high school when all the other girls wore anklets—I was humiliated. I couldn't take part in school activities, and yet when David took part in a stage production, no one stopped him." (Actually our parents never knew about David's stage performance—we kept it quiet because we were proud of our brother playing one of the lead roles in the school play titled, The Scarecrow. David received loud applause and we thought his role as the scarecrow might lead him into acting.)

We all reacted differently to these encounters with Nan. Dad seemed to have a mixture of sadness and pity and Mother became increasingly angry with her for bringing up accusations over and over, especially since Dad was sickly and she wanted to protect him from Nan's attacks on their parenting. Nothing they said seemed to appease or console Nan. My reaction was to keep out of the arguments and remain aloof. She seemed less and less a sister I wanted to know.

Nan boasted to me that she was the only one in the family who had expanded her mind beyond the narrowness of our religion through her studies of other religions, and that she had the freedom to include people of all faiths on the road to heaven. At that time, I still lived by the faith of my parents; I had not yet searched the Scripture to define and give testimony to my faith, so I remained silent.

In her later years, Nan seemed to want to be a part of the family. She admired her brother's ministry, and was astounded hearing of Mother's Coffee House ministry in Greenwich Village. She seemed more contented with herself, and proud of her accomplishments as a teacher of children with learning disabilities. But like the elder son in the story Jesus told of the Prodigal Son, I could not understand why she suddenly wanted to be part of the family. Her confrontational attitudes disturbed me; I complained to God that I could not cope with a sister I could not tolerate.

Complaining to God can often be a good prayer since God is sure to show His side of the story—which is the Truth. Using the very teaching I claimed to believe, the Holy Spirit showed me the Lord held me more responsible for my actions toward Nan than He held Nan accountable for her attitude toward the family. I had grown in the knowledge and in the security of God's love for me and I had begun to understand what it meant to love God with all my heart and mind, and my neighbor as myself. But I had not thought of Nan as being my "neighbor"—she was simply my sister who had made the family her battleground.

My decision to be obedient to the Lord and to trust Him to help me receive Nan as a sister with no strings attached, helped us both begin a friendship. She visited my home and I visited hers. We discovered that we had much in common; she wanted to redecorate her house and I had lots of magazines and ideas left over from decorating my house. We talked about our shared interest in decorating a new home. I never dug up her past, and she never referred to her past hurts. This became an ongoing way to become acquainted with each other and soon led to a deeper level of communication.

About three weeks before my sister had to be rushed to the hospital with a severe respiratory attack, Nan and I had a long and important telephone conversation about our family life and about our mother. Had it taken place earlier, it may have brought a resolution to the estrangement between Nan and Mother.

Nan had called that day to inform me she would be on a short vacation but wanted to be informed about Mother's ailing health. She requested: "Ruth, would you leave a message on my answering machine if Mother takes a turn for the worse?"

Mother had experienced several strokes and we thought she might not live much longer.

Our conversation took a sharp turn. Suddenly to my shock, Nan burst out her thoughts and feelings of despair and hopelessness admitting she had never been happy and did not have peace. I began to share a brief story of my dark days of despair, when Nan interrupted: "How did you come out of depression?" I told her it had been a slow process, but that it had begun with the words of Jesus: "You can know the Truth and the Truth will set you free." I explained I made a private study of the teachings of Jesus and the Apostles to find out how God regarded me and to discover the root of my depression.

Nan interrupted with a second question. "Give me an example of something that helped you."

A thought exploded in my mind, so I blurted it out: "Do you remember the Scripture verse about fearing God and keeping His commandments because it is our duty?" I told her that I once was afraid of offending God and thought I could never measure up to His demands, so I no longer had hope for myself. I explained to her the Truth that had dispelled my fear was learning I could never measure up to the righteousness of God, and that is why Jesus became human—he measured up for me.

Nan's reply brought tears to my eyes: "I've always been afraid of God."

"Nan," I answered gently, "I discovered that to fear God means to respect and reverence Him, and to trust Him to be a good and loving God." Nan whispered back: "I never knew that."

After I hung up the phone, I wrote out a prayer for Nan in my journal, asking God to complete the good work He had begun and to help her believe He loved her.

A few days later, when Nan called to inquire of Mother's health, I began to share about Mother's panic attacks caused by her many fears of feeling inadequate as a minister's wife, and believing she had to keep certain rules to win God approval, and how her family background set her up to be fearful of social encounters, and of her rebellion against the strict rules of our Lutheran grandparents. I told her Mother's "skate story" and of her anger with her father for not allowing her to have fun.

I felt a new understanding of Nan when she commented: "I wish I'd known Mother like you did. I could have been her friend." It seemed like a hallowed moment arranged by God; all the years of anger Nan harbored against Mother were melting away.

Three weeks later, while my husband I were on a vacation, my brother, Don, called to tell me that Nan had been diagnosed with terminal cancer and probably had only four months to live. We arranged to visit Nan together as soon as I arrived home. On the way home, Don called again on our cell phone while we were still five hours from home to tell me he had a strong urge he should go ahead to visit Nan. I would follow in a couple of days.

Don arrived at the hospital soon after Nan had been given morphine to ease the pain. She had opted for chemotherapy because, as she told her doctor, "I can't die now; I have too many things I want to do."

On arriving at her bedside, Don saw her condition and knew she would not live long. He took her hand and talked quietly to her: "Nan, this is your brother, Don. Can you hear me?" She nodded her head yes. He continued, "Nan, I want to ask you an important question. Have you made peace with God?" Again she nodded yes. Don then prayed, thanking God for receiving His child into the Kingdom. Tears trickled down Nan's checks. Don knew God had sent him as a messenger of His love and to witness for the family the majestic moment when all the angels in heaven rejoiced over a child coming home. Nan died several hours later.

For months upon waking and often during the day, I would think of Nan. The shock and grief of her sudden death brought anguish to my soul that I could not shake off. I thought of all the good times we could have had as a family, and the extraordinary contributions her talents and outgoing personality could have made in the Kingdom of God. I lamented my self-righteousness. I was no different than the Pharisees who held themselves aloof from "sinners." I felt shame and remorse.

Talking out my grief and remorse with the family helped a little. Somehow, I knew the Holy Spirit allowed me to suffer the agony of the soul to get across a message. The Lord had been patient with Nan and I hadn't. He loved her even though she rebelled against His love; I withheld my love. He did not reject Nan because of her sins, but I did. I should have known better. There are no levels of guilt—I was judged just as Nan and found guilty and I felt the weight on my conscience just as Nan had all those years.

I, too, had to make peace with God by receiving His forgiveness for my attitude toward my sister. Nan, I realized had made peace with God and received His forgiveness for her attitude toward our parents and toward her Creator. She may have had a diseased body that could not fend off death, but she had a spirit free to live forever. At last, Nan was at peace.

## CHAPTER 23

# MY STORY

My parents named me after two women of the Bible—Naomi and Ruth. I am glad they chose to call me by my second name. At an early age I was captivated by the biblical story of Ruth; she was special to God and I wanted to be special, too. Being born into the Wilkerson family provided me spiritual guidance into discovering that I, too, was special to God. I have many memories of the days in which I was shown God's plans and purposes for me—and I learned they were always for my good.

Although I was not a middle child, psychologists would probably agree the position came to me when my brothers bonded as one in their attic bedroom, and my sister, six years older than I, had no affinity for a younger sister. Mother was not physically well after my birth, and the doctor told her having another child might give her new vitality—but I didn't agree, since I had the family's attention for four years. Then brother Don became the center of attraction, taking all of Mother's time and energy, entertaining the entire family with his charming personality. Eventually he moved in with his big brothers and the "gang of three" was formed. Nan, in her search for all things worldly, warned me never to enter her bedroom lest I discover her secrets. Dad was secluded in his study and we were told to be quiet while he prepared sermons. So there I was, in the middle.

What was a middle child offered in our Pentecostal home? At a first glance it seems not much! She is left with her imagination to find her way in a holiness household. And that is exactly what I did at an early age. I became a "castle builder," using everything I saw and heard to build the place of my dreams. I sat in my castle tower looking over my small world, watching people, listening to what they said, and deciding for myself what I thought was good or bad, or what I liked or disliked, or who I trusted and who I distrusted.

Very early on I learned to "weigh" what I saw and heard, but since I belonged to the generation that was seen and not heard and had no one to confide in, I learned to tuck a lot of questions in my brain. Because I was brought up in a Pentecostal home and church and attended public school, I received a lot of unusual and interesting information.

In church, I learned about God's chosen people, the Israelites. I listened as they outwitted the Egyptians to gain freedom from slavery with some help from God; I traveled with them through the hot desert, watching God perform spectacular miracles on their behalf and listened attentively to the commands Moses read from stone tablets. I called the leaders by their first names, and picked my favorites, telling God I wanted the faith of Abraham and the heart for God like King David. I avoided the threatening voices of the prophets and did not like my father's sermons that pounded out similar warnings. For a long time, it seemed to me that I must be Jewish and that these people were my ancestors. I loved the history, but their relationship to God often scared me. One day they were on intimate speaking terms with God (through a second party), and the next day God was telling them that He had had it with them.

I was glad the celebration of Christmas came every year. The history of my "ancient family" took on a new and brighter look. Angels announced the Good News of Baby Jesus' birth; carols, not heard for a year, sounded out in church, in school and in stores—all telling us the Good News was meant for us, too. I became shrouded in the silent, holy night of Christmas Eve, and like the Jews who joyously celebrated the Feasts, I reveled in our family traditions of a decorated tree, helping my father layout a little village and train underneath the brightly lit tree with a star on top, and reverently listened to the story of Jesus' birth as if hearing it for the first time.

In the New Year, Mother would read about Jesus growing up and traveling by foot to do His Father's work. When He welcomed children as his friends, I knew I was among them. Eventually, I would read and reread these stories. Each time and each story captured my heart and imagination until all that was good and mighty became a part of what I believed and who I wanted to be. I especially pondered on the story of Ruth and Boaz—I tucked that one in my mind for further consideration as to its meaning for me. I tried to ignore Naomi's story and would never allow anyone to call me by my first name.

In school, I diligently applied myself to discovering the world God created, wondering how people made use of the creative abilities endowed upon them by their Creator. I did not see much potential in myself, although I liked to read, think deep thoughts about God and life, and in fifth grade discovered I liked to write stories. There was no one to help me develop creative thought except schoolteachers, but the curriculum did not allow for much development of talents.

The history of our nation became almost as important to me as Bible history. Long before I knew that our great-grandfather had fought in the Civil War; I was drawn to this event over and over. When I read biographies or novels of that period, each story added a new piece to my castle of dreams. There were heroes and heroines of American history comparable to those in the Bible. These were people I liked, who inspired me as had the biblical characters—people with purpose who were brave and honest. God-fearing fighters for good, who were not afraid to be pioneers in a new world.

My castle became a spiritual place deep within my soul—no one went there but God and me. There were so many wonderful building "bricks" to build with and I found delight in most of them. I valued them then; now I treasure them. These treasures are hidden in me in Scripture, hymns and choruses, sermons, prayers, and memories of godly people who were not ashamed to give testimony to their faith. The words, heard so long ago, planted truths in my mind not easily forgotten. They still give me guidance and inspiration.

Sunday school classes never had a great impact on me as some people testify to, except for Mrs. McGee's third-grade class. She had a magical way of planting seeds of truth with simple teachings on honesty, kindness, love, and peace coming from the mouth of heart figures drawn on a chalkboard. They told me what God expected of me, and how to keep a clean heart. When she prayed for us, I promised God I would keep my heart clean. In seventh grade, I wanted to be like Mrs. McGee and help third graders to understand God would help them be honest, friendly, caring, and have clean hearts. A class of girls began a teaching career for me within the Church, which has been one of my greatest joys.

By the time I reached high school days, I had made my choice to dedicate my life to being a follower of Christ. It often meant times of loneliness since I could not take part in most of the social activities in school and very few social times were offered in the church. I discovered the way to be accepted by classmates was simply to compete academically, be everyone's friend by making no judgments on their religion or character, be a good listener, and be kind. In our school yearbook, the editorial staff summed up their opinion of me: "She was consientious and true to her high principles." (Yes, they misspelled conscientious, but I still felt honored.) When asked my goal for the future, I immediately responded, "Religious work."

I had narrowed my future down to being a missionary-teacher. Our Pentecostal views on a secular education became the influencing factor for choosing to attend the denomination's Bible institute where my father served on the Board. I did not find much satisfaction at a religious school. I returned home determined to find a way to attend a secular college and prepare to be a teacher.

I thought God had provided a miracle when I received a four-year scholarship to the University of Pittsburgh, and I could not understand having to give it up and move to Scranton with my parents. Although these were brighter times for Dad in his ministry, they were disturbing times for me. It was then that I began to establish a personal journey with God, becoming less dependent on my parents for guidance and daily asking the Holy Spirit to reveal God's plans and purposes to me.

Those prayers brought Don into my life. He had always been drawn to the Church and knew about Catholic traditions, but very little about the Gospel. The teachings of a new birth and transformation greatly appealed to Don's spiritual hopes for himself, so he readily responded to the invitation to go to the altar and present himself as a sinner and receive Christ as his Savior. Don was immediately caught up in the Pentecostal tradition of considering training for church ministry. Since it was a calling I knew best and enjoyed, I agreed, even though I had decided being a pastor's wife would not be my first choice for a ministry.

While David, Don, and Mother faced the trials of establishing Teen Challenge in New York City, Don and I struggled in pastoral ministry at a small country church in North Carolina. We became church workaholics—working hard to establish a more appealing church building and to increase the membership. Don would use his new knowledge to preach his first sermons. I would be a "helpmate" as my mother had been to her husband.

My father had presented Don with a children's Bible

storybook—a gift he gave to every adult convert who had not attended Sunday school. Don took the stories of the Israelites and spun modern day stories of how to get to the Promise Land—which, for us, meant having faith to remove the large stove dominating the sanctuary and replace it with a proper furnace; and instead of cleaning the inside of the church by hosing down the walls, pews, and upright piano, we would paint the walls, refinish the pews, lay an oak floor over the worn sub-floor, and purchase a grand piano. Somehow we would do all this on a very limited budget. The people caught the vision and took pride in the transformation. Children and adults pitched in with the work—the sheer joy of each accomplishment spilled over into making the dreams they had for themselves become a reality. Don and I set an active spiritual standard for ourselves, both of us believing our works were necessary to please God and win His favor.

There would be many tests of our faith. With a small salary of twenty-five dollars a week, and a child to raise, plus a payment on a second-hand car, we were forced to depend on God. Only once did we try to provide for ourselves by taking several ears of corn from a farmer's field behind the church. We were sure he would not mind if we did a bit of "biblical gleaning." When a board member stopped by the parsonage, we told him our sad story of boiling and boiling the corn and it would not soften. He howled so long over our ignorance of not recognizing that it was feed for animals that even we had to laugh.

One event that happened to me in the parsonage reads like a biblical miracle. Don had gone to a funeral, so I took advantage of the quiet time while Karen, our two-year-old daughter napped, and made myself cozy with a good book and a blanket over my lap. A sharp pain in my left leg interrupted the story. The stiffness that began settling in prompted me to call out to God for help. An inner voice replied to my prayer: "Ruth, stand up and shake the blanket." I did and out fell a black widow spider that had been injecting its venom in my body. Later church members told me of a farmer killed by numerous spider bites. Had I not listened to the inner voice of the Spirit, I may have died—there was no hospital or doctor in the country village to come to my rescue.

When all our "works" seemed completed, we both had the urge to move to a larger community. We thought we were being honored when the State Superintendent of our denomination asked if we would pioneer a new church in a small town. It all sounded so good: the denomination would provide a loan to purchase an old Baptist church, but we had to find the resources to pay back the loan and provide an income for our needs. The offer sounded like one my father would have enthusiastically responded to, and that is exactly what we did—not "reading the fine print" behind the offer.

It didn't matter that I was pregnant with Jeffrey, our second child. Everyone, including me, expected I would keep up with my husband in the preparation of the building for a congregation that had yet to appear. With help from a young man who had been searching for a church to attend, we painted the sanctuary, scrubbed down the rooms in preparation for Sunday school, and hoped the activity would draw people to the church.

We soon discovered one reason the Baptists had built a new church. Being near sea level caused water to gather under the building and all kinds of creatures would appear. Bedroom slippers at night were a necessary tool to cope with large black water bugs. The big "worms" our children watched crawling up the outside walls turned out to be rattlesnakes. We knew the rats crawled up a drainage pipe, but we couldn't determine where the possums came from!

Those were minor trials compared to what we faced in pioneering a new church. Probably we were our own worst problem. We were too "green," not having enough sense to negotiate a salary or the promise of helpers to build up a congregation. Nevertheless, we trudged on and laid a foundation for a permanent Pentecostal church in the community.

Mother visited us after the birth of our second daughter, Laurie. She had been concerned for my physical and emotional health. She quickly realized that we were both too discouraged to keep prodding on under stressful conditions—some which showed in our marriage. She had strong words to say that reminded me of Uncle John's advice to my father: "You need to get out of here."

We heeded her advice and not long afterward we moved to Queens, a borough of New York City. My husband had been recommended to a small church by a friend. The congregation and our family began a journey that would have great highs and great lows.

After many years of isolation from Christians in other denominations and six years of living in the seclusion of small communities, New York was a huge cultural and spiritual shock. Most surprising was the discovery that my mother and brothers had gone beyond the past years when we were not only isolated from the broader Church, but also from the world. Now I was seeing firsthand the ministries of Teen Challenge, and it became very evident that my mother and brothers had been compelled by the Holy Spirit beyond the comfort of the church walls and the holiness mentality of our past. Even though our family had always taken the Gospel to the streets, David was the first one to stay on the streets. Instead of insisting converts join the Church, he made the streets the church. He went beyond leading them in the sinner's prayer—he also provided for their emotional and physical needs. This was a new way of "doing church" and one I had never seen or been part of. I felt left behind by the family and by God. Comparing my works to their work for the Lord, I felt worthless.

I did not know how to enter into greater spiritual experiences as they had, so I withdrew into my own little world just as I had always done. Only this time, the castle I had built during my childhood days had almost completely fallen apart. I had nowhere to go. The religious heritage I had loved no longer gave me comfort, or peace and security. Just like my ancient "family," I wandered in the miseries of a wilderness and believed God had brought me to the worst place of isolation I had ever experienced because of my lack of faith.

My "good works" were curtailed when our fourth child, Susan, was born and the partnership Don and I had enjoyed together in church ministry ended. While I became a stay-at-home mom, Don discovered there was little need for his administrative abilities and became restless with a small congregation mostly made up of one large extended family that seemed to have no plans for growth. It soon became noticeable that Don was stuck in his own spiritual quagmire and I could not help him.

Instead of entering a bright future in the city where Mother and my brothers had a successful ministry, I became increasingly depressed. Don and I were no longer a team working together in the Church. I had no friends and no church ministry. I felt alone, lonely, and useless. Since birth, I had only known a life within the Church. I lived and breathed the life of church activities. Those losses that I felt so deeply, troubled my soul. I imagined my husband and my God no longer cared for me and no longer valued me. I built a wall of despair and hopelessness around my heart and I could not find my way out. The shame and guilt of my spiritual confusion kept me from seeking help from my family. They, I reasoned, had enough troubled people to help at Teen Challenge. Brick by brick, my safe castle came tumbling down. I lost sight of the Gospel of peace, joy, and security—they, too, had abandoned me.

It was at this time of great emotional and spiritual confusion that my brother, Jerry, knocked on our door seeking refuge in our home, and we could only offer him a basement bedroom. The desperate place both Jerry and I were in, had seemed unthinkable in the days of being sheltered within our home and church. I believed I had disappointed God and at last He, too, had grown weary of my complaints and lack of faith. There seemed to be no reason to live.

I believed God was present with me, but He seemed silent, no longer the One alongside me to guide me or give me encouragement. Yet, whether from habit or from desperation, I continued to cry out to God to help me find the way out of the dark maze.

One day, as I sat at our piano bench staring out into space, I heard the "still, small voice" of the Holy Spirit addressing me by name: "Ruth, you can know the Truth and the Truth will set you free." His voice startled me; I hadn't expected to hear words of hope from God. A dim glimmer of light began to penetrate the darkness of my soul, and that day I determined to become a seeker for the Truth. Nothing changed between Don and me. There were no offers to do a great work for the Kingdom of God, but on the day I chose to make a spiritual journey, I also began to experience hope and a greater awareness of God's love.

Daily prayer and the study of the teachings of Jesus and the Apostles became the living force lifting me up out of despair. I had allowed good works to determine my worth; I would learn that God created me for His pleasure and loved me for who I was—not for my works. I had known of God's love for me and that He had good plans for me, but it had never occurred to me I was in a battle against the enemy of my soul. When Satan came in like a "lion," I thought it was God punishing me for not keeping all the rules. The Holy Spirit took me on a journey into the Truth—even while I still searched for satisfaction by good works.

On that spiritual journey, I made a discovery that would change almost everything I knew and thought about myself, about God and the Church. I had to admit that I had never gone beyond an elementary knowledge of God and His plans and purposes concerning me. And I became very aware that I had never entered into a close union with the Lord. I was still living back in the Barnesboro and Turtle Creek experiences! I had seen my father be a diligent student of the Word, and I knew my brothers studied the Scriptures. I had read the first chapter of The Cross and Switchblade five times, trying to figure out how David could be so close to the Lord and be used so mightily by the Holy Spirit. And yet, here I was sitting in my home depressed, thinking God had grown weary of me.

When the Holy Spirit came to me and in the quietness of my spirit showed me the reason for my spiritual wanderings, I understood He meant I was to do just as my parents and brothers had done: seek God alone, apart from my husband, my family, and other Christians. I needed to take the foundational stones I had been given in my youth and build a higher, and larger and stronger union with the Lord. He, I discovered, was the "Castle" where I could live in peace and security.

Don and I continued in the ministry doing many good works. We were involved with the Jesus Movement and the Charismatic movement in the Protestant and Catholic Churches. I found great joy and good friends when I broke through the walls of past isolations. I no longer had to seek ways to serve the Lord; He opened the doors for me to share the Truths I had been learning.

We each had high and low experiences on our journeys that led to the need to take a sabbatical from church ministry. By that time, we both realized we no longer had the passion to lead a congregation. God miraculously opened another ministry for Don in health care administration. The many stresses of church ministry on our marriage and family, and the darkness of our hearts lifted as we chose to continue our spiritual journey.

* * *

Family and friends meeting around the throne of God is not

idle speculation. It is a promise given to every believer and seen in a revelation given to Apostle John—one that our parents believed would happen in time and space—a real, live event! It is there each one of us will give an account of how we lived our life on earth.

We will be questioned by our Creator: Did we believe God? Did we trust in the resurrection power of Christ to make us a new creation? Did we devote our lives to Christ or did we live selfishly, ignoring the love and rule of God? Did we live in obedience to the Holy Spirit as He revealed God's will and purposes for our life on earth? Did we offer our lives as a living sacrifice to do the works of Christ?

These are the questions asked of every generation. They are questions asked of our family. Each generation that has gone before us has proved to be faithful to God. It has been our turn to prove faithful. I believe that we have. And I am confident the Holy Spirit will plant the same faith in the generations coming after us and they, too, will be found faithful.

Someday we will meet the patriarchs and the long list of lineage that pioneered farms, towns, and churches, and created Christian homes. We will meet to talk about the wonderful works of God that we were privileged to be part of through our journey on earth. What a Wilkerson reunion that will be!

# EPILOGUE

While writing about my family, our history became something more to me than a collection of stories. The common thread weaving its way through each family was very evident: we are families with a strong sense of purpose and we strive to fulfill the call to be a righteous people and to do good works. Each person has had his or her own particular calling and acted upon it according to his or her faith in God.

We have discovered that the Spirit will breathe life upon our mustard-seed-size faith until we are empowered to believe and act beyond our human limitations. But there is a cost to living a life in the Spirit—we must surrender ourselves to His will and purposes to become an extraordinary people. Throughout our family lineage there have been people of great faith because they took God's word literally and acted upon God's commands and promises.

And yet, I know we are a very ordinary family. I have written about our strengths and weaknesses that make up the common thread which has never been broken. I have noticed that in spite of our ordinariness and lack of "sainthood," God has never abandoned our family—He keeps calling us to be a righteous people. He keeps endowing us with faith to work for His Kingdom. Our family has dared to believe this way of life is God's plan for us.

Our legacy has only been possible because God's hand has been upon our family. The miracle is that we have recognized we are a chosen people. And as with the ancient Israelites called to reveal God's plans for the world, God has allowed each generation to be tested and tried. But when we come through the fires of life, we have "gold" in our hands, and we are compelled by the Spirit to share this treasure with the world.

The gold is the gift of faith that stirs us to believe God. When we believe God, our faith is increased, and when faith grows deeper in our hearts, we are able to believe the Holy Spirit will empower us to do greater works. This, I believe, is how God can take the ordinary person and make them extraordinary.

Yes, I have been profoundly moved by the stories of each generation, but I have been more deeply affected by knowing they endured the fires of life and came through with precious gold. They have taken what God has gifted to them and shared it with the world. The generations who have found rest and reward in heaven have inspired me to refine the gold that I have been given and dare to believe God has chosen me to share this treasure.

It is important for each generation to know the God who will walk through the fire with them, so that they too can have gold in their hands to offer the world. If they will listen for the voice of God calling them to His Kingdom to become extraordinary people by the power of the living Christ, they will be the Light in a world of darkness. This is the Wilkerson Legacy waiting to be taken up by the present and the future generations of our family.